SCHOOLS:
THEY HAVEN'T
GOT A PRAYER

SCHOOLS: THEY HAVEN'T GOT A PRAYER

Lynn R. Buzzard

David C. Cook Publishing Co.

ELGIN, ILLINOIS—WESTON, ONTARIO

ABOUT THE AUTHOR

Lynn R. Buzzard is executive director of the Christian Legal Society, a national organization of Christian lawyers. He is host of "Benchmark," a daily three-minute report on law and liberty that is aired on radio stations throughout the country. Lynn also serves as coeditor of the *Religious Freedom Reporter,* a professional legal journal that reports on religious liberty cases.

Mr. Buzzard taught in a private elementary school and also taught social studies in a public high school. For seven years he taught practical theology at Northern Baptist Seminary.

He is coauthor of *Battle for Religious Liberty* and *Tell It to the Church* and editor of *Freedom and Faith.*

Lynn Buzzard received his undergraduate degree in history and graduate degrees in education and theology at Duke University, did his doctoral work in law and theology at San Francisco Theological Seminary, and has studied at Notre Dame College of Law and DePaul College of Law.

ACKNOWLEDGMENTS

Sections from the book *My Life without God,* by William J. Murray, are reprinted by permission of the Thomas Nelson Publishers. Copyright © 1982 by William J. Murray.

Excerpt from "School Prayers: A Common Danger," by John Warwick Montgomery, © 1982 *Christianity Today,* are used by permission.

Excerpts from "I Teach the Bible in a Public School," (*Christian Herald,* September 1982) © 1982 Joyce Vedral, are used by permission.

SCHOOLS: THEY HAVEN'T GOT A PRAYER
© 1982 Lynn R. Buzzard

Published by David C. Cook Publishing Co., Elgin, Il 60120.
Cover design by Britt Taylor Collins.
Edited by Janet Hoover Thoma and Susan Miriam Zitzman.
Printed in the United States of America.

Library of Congress Cataloging in Publication Data

Buzzard, Lynn Robert.
  Schools: they haven't got a prayer.

  Bibliography: p.
  1. Schools—United States—Prayers.
2. Church and state—United States.
I. Title.
BV283.S3B89   1982   322'.1'0973   82-14436
ISBN 0-89191-713-6

Printed in the United States of America.
ISBN 0-89191-713-6
LC: 82-14436

CONTENTS

PART ONE
WHY NOT A LITTLE OL' TIME RELIGION?

1

An Issue
Without an Amen

Schools: they haven't got a prayer, it seems—literally! And this is more of a problem than you may realize. For twenty years the courts and local school officials have wrestled with the meaning of the First Amendment in relation to religion in the public classroom. And the results have often made Christians wonder what has happened to their religious freedom. . . .

For instance, in November of 1981, the Tennessee attorney general declared that coaches who allowed school football players to have group prayers before or after practices or games were violating the First Amendment's prohibition against the establishment of religion.

The coach of Warren County High School quickly replied that he would defy the attorney general. His team would continue to pray, he vowed, until "there's a bunch of federal marshals with guns around." Even the Tennessee State Board of Education commended coaches who ignored the attorney general's unusual order. One board member, Hugh McDade, declared, "We don't pay any attention to the attorney general most of the time. I don't see why we should start now."[1]

Coaches from two teams openly defied the attorney general at the end of a play-off football game in Nashville, Tennessee. The two teams gathered in the middle of the field to say the Lord's Prayer. In our secular world, prayer after a football game—instead of beer and loud catcalls—might seem sissy or quaint. In this case the action called for Marine-style fortitude.

Students in other parts of the country have also been denied their religious freedom.

A small group of students at Guilderland High School in New York State asked the principal if they could meet for prayer in a classroom before school started. Not only did the principal say no, the local court and the court of appeals agreed. In fact, the court of appeals said such practices would be "too dangerous to permit."

Even teachers have been reprimanded.

Gaylord Anderson, a teacher in Council Bluffs, Iowa, led students and teachers in prayer at school assembly programs that celebrated Easter and Christmas. Another teacher, Milton Abramson, and the Iowa Civil Liberties Union sued Gaylord Anderson for $6,000, because of the "emotional distress" Abramson felt after being exposed to school prayer. The court upheld Abramson's protest, though it noted that the teacher's distress was "of short duration" and reduced the award to $300. Mr. Abramson declared that he hoped his victory would be a "deterrent to stop these kinds of things."

Education. Religion. Children. The public is so sensitive about these areas that no one seems ready to say "Amen" about prayer and religious instruction in the schools. And as the nation faces increasing internal problems, the question of our nation's moral and spiritual status becomes more and more of a political concern.

So much so that presidential candidate Ronald Reagan asked in 1979, "Where were we when God was expelled from the classroom?"[2] He promised to do something about this expulsion—and in 1982 he fulfilled that pledge. His timing was perfect: May 6, the day set aside by Congress as a National Day of Prayer.

"This Administration will soon submit to the United States Congress a proposal to amend our Constitution to allow our children to pray in school," Reagan announced to a crowd of supporters in the White House Rose Garden.

Ironically, one of the honored guests at the ceremony that afternoon was William Murray, the thirty-five-year-old son of noted atheist Madalyn Murray O'Hair. William, who had been the plaintiff in one of the major cases that struck prayer and Bible reading from the schools in 1963 (*Murray* v. *Curtlett*), declared, "I will direct all my energies toward restoring religious liberties to the schools . . . which I helped rob them of.''

To some one-hundred-twenty religious and conservative political leaders gathered there, Reagan said, ''No one will ever convince me that a moment of voluntary prayer will harm a child or threaten a school or state. But I think it can strengthen our faith in a Creator who alone has the power to bless America.''

Reagan said the amendment would fit the intent of the Constitution, which was not to ''protect us from religion,'' but to ''protect religion from government tyranny.'' He lamented that ''in recent years well-meaning Americans, in the name of freedom, have taken freedom away. For the sake of religious tolerance, they've forbidden religious practice in our public classrooms.''

Clearly Reagan disagreed with former president Jimmy Carter, who, though a professing Christian, had reacted to other efforts to reintroduce school prayers by suggesting that the government ''ought to stay out of the prayer business.''[3]

The constitutional amendment Reagan later proposed states:

> Nothing in this Constitution shall be construed to prohibit individual or group prayer in public schools or other public institutions. No person shall be required by the United States or by any state to participate in prayer.

REACTIONS

The ''heart cry'' of the American people may have helped to ''jar things loose,'' observed Cecil Todd, who was present in the Rose Garden and had earlier delivered to the White House fifty mailbags of petitions bearing a million names of those who favored voluntary prayer in the schools.

''This time Madalyn Murray O'Hair must not win!'' declared Jerry Falwell, president of the Moral Majority. He called May 6, 1982, a ''bright day in America . . . the light at the end of the tunnel.'' And the May 24 issue of the *Moral Majority Report* announced, ''The Nation Welcomes Plan to Restore Public School Prayer.'' A message from Falwell declared, ''Now is our golden opportunity to get prayer back into our school systems. We may never have a chance like this again. . . .

After 20 years of the expulsion of Almighty God from our public schools, we have the opportunity we have hoped, worked and prayed so long for." The back page featured a "prayer ballot" for supporters to voice their opinion to their congressmen.

Another spokesman for the Moral Majority, Cal Thomas, noted the explosion in vandalism, drug use, and unwanted pregnancies among our youth. We can observe for ourselves whether the removal of prayer "has been a blessing or a curse to young people," he said. "If liquor by the drink and pornography is OK, why not prayer? Is prayer more dangerous?" he queried. "It's time to resist the efforts of the American Civil Liberties Union (ACLU) who have "conducted a religious lobotomy on this country," seeking to strip it of "any vestige of religious influence."

Many saw the amendment as a way to encourage schools who had been frightened by court rulings on prayer and religious influence. The courts "have intimidated every person who wants to pray," declared evangelist James Robison. Bill Bright, president of Campus Crusade for Christ International, had noted in earlier testimony to Congress: Children "can say 'god damn' but they can't say 'God be praised' " in school.

And in June of 1982, the 13.6 million member Southern Baptist Convention became the first Protestant body to support the Reagan proposal.

NOT ALL WERE CHEERING!

But the opponents were not asleep. At a press conference the same day as Reagan's speech, religious and other groups that have traditionally opposed school prayers voiced their concerns. Some, like Marc Pearl of the American Jewish Congress, claimed that no amendment was needed for voluntary prayers anyway, so why "junk up the Constitution with an unnecessary law."

James M. Dunn, executive director of the Baptist Joint Committee on Public Affairs, seemed to agree with Pearl, declaring that the Supreme Court has never banned prayer—and furthermore, it can't! Dunn called the president's proposal "despicable demagoguery," since he believed it was really playing "petty politics with prayer." *Commonweal,* the conservative magazine, called the proposal a "political IOU to a religious constituency.''[4] Some skeptics suggested it was Reagan's attempt to take the nation's focus off troubles with the economy.

Six religious groups, including the National Council of Churches, the Baptist Joint Committee on Public Affairs, and several Jewish groups said the whole attempt to introduce religious practices into the public schools would likely generate the very kind of ''interreligious tension and conflict'' that the writers of the First Amendment wished to prevent.

Some religious leaders hedged their bets. The Reverend Myron Augsburger, a prominent Mennonite leader and pastor in Washington, D.C., said, ''I'm a little uncomfortable with the idea . . . it depends on whether it's clear that prayer can't be required of anybody.'' The evangelical magazines *Christianity Today* and *Eternity* carried articles questioning the value of the theologically vague public school prayers that the amendment could elicit.

TEMPEST IN A TEAPOT?

Will the school prayer issue again become a major religious and political debate? Some suggest that Congress will neither have the will nor the time to struggle with the emotionally charged prayer question. The budget and international affairs will claim all its energies. Others predict that Congress will call for some hearings, but in the end the issue will likely die where almost all other prayer amendment proposals have—in committee.

However, some anticipate serious battle in the face of the political strength of the new conservative element in the nation. Jon Garth Murray, William Murray's brother and a vigorous supporter of his mother's anti-God crusade, said the battle is now set in Congress. He feared that if the amendment passed in Congress, it would roll easily through the states.

WHAT DOES IT MEAN?

A good many observers wonder: Just what does the Reagan proposal protect or assure? The amendment, by noting that no one would be required to participate, focuses on ''voluntary'' prayer, but what does voluntary mean?

Webster defines *voluntary* as ''proceeding from the will or from one's own choice or consent,'' but in the instance of classroom prayer the individual's choice is muddied by other factors. One commentator doubted the ability of children to resist "subtle pressure from their peers to participate."[5]

Administration spokesmen said the amendment's intention was to restore the nation's practices before the Supreme Court struck down school prayer in 1962.

But were these pre-1962 prayers voluntary? The Court decisions in *Engel* v. *Vitale* and *Abington* v. *Schempp*, the major prayer cases, each involved a state-prescribed prayer led by a teacher. The only voluntary aspect was that a student could choose not to participate.

Reagan's amendment could promote a broader sort of voluntarism, in which the prayers would occur during school time, but the students would voluntarily write and lead the prayers. The amendment might even focus on a right that is now being denied: students' ability to gather in a room before school to pray.

It could be that the language is purposely vague so that it can accommodate any one of these options. However, the president's remarks as he announced the amendment referred to "religious practice in our public classrooms." This seems to imply group prayer in an actual classroom situation, with the school providing for and perhaps initiating the activity, and allowing the right of nonparticipation.

Certainly Congress will attempt to clarify the language if it does seriously consider the issue.

A CHRISTIAN VIEW?

It is clear from the reactions to the president's proposal that not all Christians agree on the wisdom of amending the Constitution in this way. Some apparently see it as a tremendous opportunity to reverse the course of our nation and restore essential values and faith to our collapsing society. Others, equally committed to the Lordship of Christ, are disturbed by the involvement of government in any religious activity, especially in so sensitive an area as prayer with children. They see pluralism as a legitimate character for the state.

Should Christians support the amendment? What would voluntary prayer accomplish in the secular school program? And what about the whole direction of education today? Doesn't the explosion of educational secularism demand a response that would reinstate values in public education?

The prayer amendment issue may raise a public debate about these most essential and urgent issues, which call for answers not simply from Christians but from society at large.

However, this debate will totally fail if it only instigates inflammatory rhetoric and attacks by both sides; the one side labeled as "New Right Neanderthals" seeking to destroy liberties and impose their views on civilization. The other: "fuzzy headed liberals and atheists" out to destroy our American heritage. I propose that we carefully consider these issues—now, before it is too late.

2

The Tragic Litany

Come mothers and fathers
Thoughout the land
And don't criticize
What you can't understand.
Your sons and your daughters
Are beyond your command
Your old road is
Rapidly aging!
Please get out of the new one
If you can't lend your hand
For the times they are a-changin'.

This verse of Bob Dylan's song, "The Times They Are A-Changin'," written in 1963, was observant and also prophetic of American culture. But whereas Dylan hoped the changes he wrote of would bring love, peace, and justice to our land, in retrospect we might well ask if any improvement has been made. Another observer, noted psychiatrist Norman O. Brown, pronounced, "The survival of man is a utopian hope."

Indeed, both Dylan and Brown seem to be right. Can anyone deny the changes or the tragedy? The explosion of nuclear arms. The acceleration of crime, drug abuse, and a bold and vicious pornography.

Frank Goble in his volume *Beyond Failure* notes the dimensions of the problems in a tragic litany:

> Alcoholism, suicide, illegitimacy, venereal disease, broken marriages; inflation, unemployment, debt, increasing taxes; an energy crisis, resource depletion, environmental deterioration; shoplifting, vandalism, fraud and corruption in business and government, militant unions; urban blight, bankrupt city treasuries, excessive bureaucratic regulations; and high welfare rolls and expenditures—all of these are symptoms of social disintegration.[1]

No wonder University of Illinois Professor Edward Wynne's research has noted a steady deterioration in the attitudes of young people toward society since about 1950.[2]

The drug problem alone is staggering. The Department of Justice pointed to a 1,288 percent increase from 1960 to 1972, and in 1973 the United States House Select Committee on Crime reported that "the drug crisis in our schools greatly exceeded our worst expectations." They noted it is "infecting and contaminating our schools and leaving a trail of devastation."[3]

We are in a crisis. The survival of our nation may not be at stake, but one surely wonders if we shall have a culture at all by the year 2,000. The issue of school prayer has not emerged in a vacuum. In fact it is only the tip of the iceberg. The revived interest in school prayer cannot be separated from the emergence of public debates about a host of issues with moral dimensions: abortion, parental rights, sexual mores, and homosexuality.

In fact, the attraction of school prayer as a perennial issue may be precisely because of its capacity to symbolize this larger struggle over the character of culture and society and the role of moral and religious values in our public life. Rabbi Juda Glasner of the Union of Orthodox Rabbis expressed this belief in his testimony before Congress:

> I declare that the urgency to reaffirm the undeniable right of an avowal of faith has been heightened due to the critical times . . . and the ever increasing moral laxity.[4]

Glasner went on to quote Deuteronomy 31:17: "And many evils and troubles shall befall them; so that they will say in that day, Are not these evils come upon us, because our God is not among us?"

The cultural crisis is, I believe, real and profound. Where is the moral leadership for the crises of Iran, Ireland, the Middle East, or the South Pacific? Where is the prophetic leadership that speaks to the emptiness in our youth? The crime in our communities?

"Matters have gotten out of hand," says Pulitzer Prize-winning novelist Saul Bellow, noting the violence in our whole society. It is so bad, Bellow insists, that we try to "cancel horror after horror" as we become increasingly "used to brutality and savagery. Where are the answers?" Bellow wonders. We turned to the experts: those intellectuals who were "trained in departments of education or social service administration or psychology, but they didn't know how to deal with the big human questions." In fact, "nobody knows how to deal with them." So we all participate in a scheme of evasion, expelling the struggle from our consciousness. We focus on the minutiae of life, pretending it is real. We have become enamored with freedom, and its abuse has meant chaos. The end result? "We are divested of the deeper human meaning . . . lives don't have any meaning. . . . There's no sacred space . . . the feeling that life is sacred has died away in this century."[5]

THE EMERGENCE OF MORALITY AS A POLITICAL ISSUE

A researcher conducting a study on the character of our society by the Connecticut Mutual Life Insurance Company noted, "Something unusual is happening here. Moral issues through religion have vaulted to the forefront of political dialogue."

Part of this "something unusual" is the emergence of the religious community—and especially persons and groups who were once content in their comfortable pews and their cloisters—to hit the political trails and become activists, essayists, demonstrators, and lobbyists. These activists agree with many observers that our nation is undergoing a profound and deep moral crisis, one that reveals the lack of any informing ethic. Our materialism, hedonism, existentialism, and pragmatism have done us in. There is an emptiness in the soul of the nation and its people, an image common in modern literature. Certainly it is a theme of the works of Camus, Orwell, Kesey, and countless others.

Is it any wonder that there is a reaction in the religious and political communities? David Reisman, noted sociologist, suggests a corrective action might mean that "we could be in for another period of profound transformation."[6] Could it be a return to more conservative moral and religious values?

Still the new energy of the so-called "new right" has created a storm of protest. It is ironic that so many religious groups with long-standing traditions of political involvement have charged the new right with violating some sacred trust when it became politically involved. Earlier, the conservative right was inactive politically. Richard Neuhaus, project director of the Council on Religion and International Affairs, remembers, "By the end of the 1920s, fundamentalism had been expelled from the circles of the influential and respectable, and in truth, retreated almost faster than it could be expelled. . . . It would not be heard from again for 40 years. The mainline was left in secure possession of all the religious turf that mattered—or so the mainline thought. In exile, fundamentalism . . . set about building an alternative 'righteous empire.' Fundamentalism had lost touch with the elite, but not with millions of believers." Neuhaus notes that recently "some mainline Protestants began to wonder whether *they* were now the ones in exile."

"Typical of the mainline," Neuhaus says, "is *Engage/Social Action,* a United Methodist magazine, whose 1980 pre-election issue blasted Moral Majoritarians for saying that there is a Christian position on many public issues. The same issue carried a comparison of the Democratic, Republican, and Anderson platforms with the official teachings of the United Methodist church. It turns out that the church's positions are those of the Democratic party, and any differences would have been reconciled had the party's McGovern-Kennedy wing written the entire platform."[7]

One United Methodist minister, writing in a Methodist publication, called the involvement of the new right "both dangerous and pathetic." The secretary of Health, Education, and Welfare in the Carter administration compared the new right to the "religious zealots of Iran" and wondered if there was an ayatollah in this country. Bishop James Armstrong, the new president of the National Council of Churches (NCC), warned his constituency of the danger the Moral Majority poses to our country. And the Reverend John Swonley, a theologian and head of the ACLU's church-state committee, called the new right a "neo-fascist threat."

As one commentator notes, the new right has not yet been blamed for the medfly plague in California, but there's still time!

Norman Lear has now organized his People of the American Way as a counterforce to Moral Majority and other religious elements of the new right. *Commonweal,* a Jesuit magazine, has already taken Lear to task for adopting the tactics he accuses Falwell of.[8]

Some columnists have noted the irony of all these attacks. Kevin Phillips, a syndicated columnist, was particularly acerbic:

> The new Christian conservatives are coming under frantic fire from many of the same liberal ministers, priests and rabbis who spent the bulk of the 1960's and the early 70's turning their churches and synagogues into staging areas for sit-ins, busing rallies, marijuana legalization fronts, anti-war rallies, Ho Chi Minh fund-raisers and "damn South Africa" meetings. This ilk wrote books trying to wrap Christianity around the extremities of the progressive chic, and now they have the nerve to stand up and voice pious outrage at the attempt of the Christian right to link their faith with a brand of politics.[9]

Perhaps some of the distress over prayer in school is a reaction to the fact that it is supported by this new right. Could it be a sign that a moral change might take place? Or that the new right might now dominate the religious and political scene?

Certainly many people are beginning to wonder how long a society can draw upon the credit of its history. As William Barrett of the National Humanities Center declared recently, "pluralism is a good thing . . . yet it seems a nation requires a central core of values." And as if the threats of the present are not enough, one wonders where the resources to deal with the profound ethical issues posed by the current revolution in genetics will come from. Who will control man-made human life? A national corporation now owns a patent to produce human cells. One wonders what they will create.

How does a two-minute school prayer fit in with all of this? Does it become all the more urgent in light of our current moral chaos? Or is it too little too late?

The noted Nobel Prize-winning geneticist George Beadle observed that "unlike biological inheritance, our cultural inheritance begins anew" with each generation.[10] What will this generation give as an inheritance to the next? And what are we teaching the next generation in our nation's school systems?

THE CRISIS IN EDUCATION: A FALLEN IDOL?

The school is as American as Norman Rockwell. It conjures up images of happy children meeting with loving teachers in a small frame building to learn their "readin', writin', and 'rithmetic." Never mind that such a school hardly exists anymore. This is the image, the myth. Few social institutions are the recipients of as much hope and money as the public schools. Our laws compel attendance, and our ideology lauds the school as the source of our future and assurance of our democracy. We have idolized the little red schoolhouse and lauded those who have given themselves to the nurture of the young. Education is surely part of the American dream.

Approximately 65 million Americans are involved in education, either as students or teachers, and the costs perhaps run as much as $130,000,000,000 a year.[11] With all this investment of people, dollars, and ideology, why is the experiment in public education so often inadequate and inept? Have we expected too much?

In fact, the image of public education is apparently so bad that some educators feel they need a "handy dandy refuter" to defend themselves. An article in *Education Digest,* "Do Schools Stink? Why Not Quote the Sweet Facts," claimed to be a "handy dandy refuter of bad news about education." However, most of us sense that it will take more than a "handy dandy refuter" to deal with the massive problems in modern education.

The issues in education today are really not about prayer.

The question is not whether or not to add some religious component. The basic and most pressing issues are about the very character of public education: where is it going and what values are shaping the philosophy of modern education?

THE QUEST FOR ALTERNATIVES

For a variety of reasons some people have already given up on public education. The explosive growth of private schools in the United States in recent years is perhaps the loudest and most concrete index of the level of discontent with public schools. What is especially striking is that much of this growth has come from a sector that has had little historic commitment to private schools: white, Protestant, middle-class Americans.

There is also a growing number of parents who have withdrawn their children entirely from formal schools and have opted to educate them at home. The movement is large enough to have a newsletter and a national organization, the National Association of Home Educators. Raymond and Dorothy Moore promote this concept in *Home Grown Kids,* with an introduction by noted family counselor James Dobson. Legislation has even been introduced or enacted in several states specifically to provide for home education, although other state boards of education are suing these parents for truancy.

Some critics have even suggested the abolition of public education, claiming that it is so counterproductive it inhibits learning. The problems are neither few nor simple. I will mention the most obvious.

Violence

Every month of the year, 280,000 students and 5,200 teachers are physically assaulted. Some 2,300,000 students and 128,000 teachers are robbed each year. On an average day 2,000,000 students in the United States are on suspension for assault, vandalism, or other violent acts. Altogether, $200,000,000 worth of vandalism occurs, according to a National Institute of Education study.[12]

Believe it or not, corporal punishment may even be making a comeback. After a five-year ban, it has been reintroduced in Los Angeles schools.[13]

"We've lost a commitment to disciplined learning," argues Terrell Bell, the secretary of education. The single most important priority in education is discipline. He insists that this is more than student behavior; it includes academic mastery of learning.

Academic Failure

Authors such as Rudolf Flesh speak of the "scandal of our schools" and "mass miseducation." The statistics are not encouraging: dropping Scholastic Aptitude Test (SAT) scores and increasing dropout rates. Across the country one-in-twelve students is absent on a given day, and in New York and Boston it's one in five.

Students are suffering "from a delusion of adequacy," according to Paul Copperman who has spoken of education as "The Literacy Hoax." He accuses the schools of becoming "the most expensive babysitting mechanism in the history of civilization." It is a "sick 130 billion dollar a year social institution . . . enormously damaging to our children."[14]

One young man who graduated in 1972 from a San Francisco high school even sued the school system for malpractice. He had been unable to do the minimal paperwork required in his jobs. He was tested and discovered his reading was at the fifth grade level. His suit charged that he should not have been passed along from grade to grade; by lying to his parents about his progress, school officials had prevented him from getting needed remedial help. The California courts dismissed his complaints.

"Are the Public Schools About to Flunk?" asked a *U.S. News and World Report* article in June of 1981. It noted a surge of interest in alternatives to traditional public schools and insisted that parents, from inner cities to the suburbs, are telling school officials, "Shape up and start teaching our children or we will abandon you." In fact Jay Parker, president of the Lincoln Institute for Research and Education, insists that the only thing that will reform education is "competition with private institutions that deliver a better product."[15] Albert Shanker, president of the American Federation of Teachers, says if the schools don't alter their ways, they will "go the way of the United States automobile to second-class status."

Beleaguered Bureaucracy

Some of the complaints revolve around the loss of parental

control and the abdication of educational policymaking to state bureaucracies and educator unions. The Heritage Foundation has been sharply critical, and Onalee McGraw, their education specialist, laments the layers of bureaucracy that create self-interest but little action. "There is a constant shifting of personal responsibility, and no one cares about educating the kids."

Educators feel threatened by a host of developments from tuition tax credits and voucher plans that will help offset the cost of private education to parental activism on such matters as textbooks and curriculum materials. Educators and teachers respond by forming lobbies, which sometimes advocate policies that undermine good education.

The education lobbies are powerful bodies. Yet the *New Republic* in its April 18, 1981 edition carried an article claiming that "nearly every necessary step to high quality education is being fought by, of all people, the nation's largest teacher's union (NEA)."[16]

Many believe the educationalists have largely ignored the failing system they are a part of. When reports showed that for fourteen straight years SAT scores had declined, a *Washington Post* headline decried, "Educators Largely Ignoring Declining Student Achievement." The accompanying article declared that the powerful educational organizations have chosen "not to assume a leadership role in a search for causes of the decline."[17]

In fact, the National Education Association seems to be getting extremely sensitive to criticism. The association in May 1982 sued Suzanne Clark, a former English professor, for $100,000 because of a letter she wrote that appeared as a column in the *Bristol Herald Courier* in Tennessee. Mrs. Clark accused the NEA of advocating "one-world government, the abolition of religion other than humanism, sexual license and drug use."[18] Clark backs up her charges with excerpts from NEA publications, such as "the school has emerged as the agency best equipped to help young people learn to live comfortably with the evolving sexual ethic of the adult world," and "[some parents and citizens] whose personal attitudes are warped . . . may complain or try to sabotage the [sex education] program."[19]

The NEA charged that Clark's statements were untrue and libelous, and would cost them both membership and status in the community. Clark refused to back down and in June 1982 filed her answer to the complaint, defending the validity of her statements, and added a counterclaim alleging infringement on her right to express her personal views on an issue of public debate.

If so many are unhappy and dissatisfied with public education today, how did this state of affairs come about? The general American consensus about the purposes, goals, and methods of education has dissolved in recent years, and parents and educators are often poles apart on such issues as the teaching of morality. In response to the terrifying results of today's public education, many parents are asking: What's going on in the classroom? What should go on? It may be that more is missing than two-minute prayers.

3
What's Going On
In the Classroom?

It has become increasingly popular in recent years for teachers to use the questions and exercises in Sidney Simon's *Values Clarification* handbook to help their students become aware of their own beliefs. The aim of the text sounds noble: to "help students become aware of the beliefs and behaviors they prize," rather than instilling a "particular set of values" by "preaching and moralizing."[1]

But the materials also "encourage students to consider alternative modes of thinking." Many parents will wonder about some of the alternatives offered, or at least question the timing for certain topics. For example, the handbook rates the following question as appropriate for all ages: "Do you like to look at pictures of nude women/men?"[2]

What's going on in the classroom, anyway? Who is to decide, in our pluralistic society, what values are taught to schoolchildren? Let us look objectively at some of the complaints and areas of conflict.

LITERATURE AND TEXTBOOKS

Who determines what children should read? The school board? The state? The government? In June of 1982 the Supreme Court did little to clarify the issue in its highly divided decision, *Pico* v. *Island Trees Union Free School District*. The Court returned to the district court a case involving whether or not the local school board was within its powers to remove certain books it found "anti-Semitic," "anti-Christian," and "just plain filthy" (including *Soul on Ice* and *Slaughterhouse Five*).

Students in the school sued, charging that the "irrationality and roughshod emotionalism of the book-banning left teachers, students, and members of the community intimidated."

At first the students' complaint was dismissed, but the Tenth Circuit Court of Appeals reversed this dismissal. The appeals court said that the school board's criteria seemed excessively general and overbroad and suggested an attempt to "express an official policy with regard to God and country." A trial was warranted to "determine precisely what happened [and] why it happened." When this decision was appealed to the Supreme Court, the Court (which was badly split on the issue) returned the case to the trial court to hear the evidence the Tenth Circuit Court had suggested.

At the time this book was written the outcome of the court's investigation had not been revealed. However, I would hope that courts in our country will listen carefully to parents' objections to school materials. Once in a while parental committees have sought to ban literature of classic proportions from school libraries and from classroom study. But there still remains legitimate question about the values present in much of public education today.

Two types of objections to literature are common. The first is specifically objectionable content: offensive words such as profanity or sexually explicit or coarse language and the inclusion of undue violence or criminal conduct. This approach examines the instruments—the words—of the educational process.

The second objection is far more difficult to ascertain and prove, but even more basic: the philosophic content and the underlying assumptions of school textbooks. The language in such materials might be quite inoffensive. But what concepts are being taught? Often the ultimate goals of a curriculum are more explicitly found in the teacher's manual. If a parent senses that an underlying concept is amoral or antireligious, it is wise to look at the directions in the manual.

In Colorado, one state representative, Republican Bob Stephenson who is chairman of the Colorado House Education Committee, has undertaken to check textbooks himself. He wrote to all of his state's 181 school districts, asking them for a list of their curriculum materials. His effort has drawn fire from some sources, and even his own district, School District 11, indicated it did not intend to comply. Stephenson has already been critical of some of the books he did receive, claiming, for example, that a seventh grade book, *Action,* consisted largely of stories about death, dying, or suicide.

Finally, take a close look at the curriculum *Man: A Course of Study* (MACOS). This fifth-grade, social science curriculum was prepared by the National Science Foundation under a government grant of over seven million dollars. Critics find it significant that a course on *man* should have only one unit on humans and preceding units on the salmon, the herring gull, and the baboon.

It doesn't take a scientist to ascertain the relativism present in such a collection. The only human culture surveyed is that of the Netsilik Eskimos, whose practices of cannibalism, wife-sharing, and abandonment of their aged are uncritically noted. The project director explains in the teacher's manual that one objective of MACOS is for children to understand that what we regard as "acceptable behaviour is a product of our culture." The study is supposed to encourage a "question[ing] of the notion that there are 'eternal truths' about humanity."[3]

VALUES CLARIFICATION

Another educational tool parents are concerned about is values clarification, and their concern is shared by the *Wall Street Journal.* "Whether intended or not, adolescents were in effect given the message that parents, the school or society had no right to tell them what standards should guide sexual behaviour."[4] More than three-hundred thousand teachers have attended workshops on values clarification techniques, and six thousand school systems have offered values programs.

Promoted initially in the mid-sixties by social scientists (most notably Sidney Simon), the concept of seeking to help students clarify their values without "indoctrinating" or trying to teach "correct" values became a widely promoted and hailed technique. It was used extensively in schools and by private groups such as Planned Parenthood, and teacher workshops promoted it.

As Richard Baer, the author of the *Wall Street Journal* article, noted, parents began to react when their children came home discussing when it might be right to lie or disobey their parents. The reaction was—and continues to be—vigorous. Some, frequently Christians, complain that the method represents a profound ethical relativism. Baer noted that these charges often meet countercharges from school and educational authorities that simply label the opponents as "simplistic" or "anti-intellectual."

But not all the objections have been from parents or the so-called new right. According to Baer, it is not only the alleged "unprogressive" parents who are critical of values clarification techniques, but also some members of the professional educational community. The critics, including the chairman of the National Endowment for the Humanities, William Bennett, and professors from schools such as the University of Wisconsin and the University of Michigan, have pointed out that values clarification is not as value neutral as its advocates claim. William Bennett and Edwin Delattre, president of St. John's College in Annapolis, claim the whole approach "emphatically indoctrinates—by encouraging and even exhorting the student to narcissistic self-gratification."[5]

The assumption that values are essentially subjective equates values with personal tastes and preferences, rejecting any standard for such judgments other than individual choice. Thus the student or child can reject another's values, such as those of parents, simply by pointing out that those are "your" values and not "mine."

Professor Alan Lockwood of the University of Wisconsin claims that the approach also constitutes a threat to family and student privacy, because of probing inquiries, which ask students to reveal their innermost selves. The pressure for self-disclosure arises from the "projective" techniques, in which students complete sentences such as "I feel guilty when . . ." and "My parents usually . . ."

Many insist that the whole approach of values clarification amounts to a religious perspective, which competes with other religious views such as biblical perspectives. The system teaches that the student is the final arbiter of truth, and that the good life is one of self-actualization and fulfillment—all notions profoundly religious in character and directly contradictory to traditional Judeo-Christian perspectives. Baer even claims the use of such techniques is so religious that it constitutes a violation of the First Amendment's prohibition against the establishment of religion.[6]

Reaction to values clarification techniques has even resulted in some proposed legislation. In Wisconsin, for example, a proposal (Assembly Bill 521), would require the informed, written consent of a student's parent before the child could participate in a public school program whose purpose modifies the child's behavior or the personal values of the family and their moral preferences. The bill would also limit the power of the school to engage in psychological testing and restrict attempts by the schools to gain personal information from a student about the student's family activities, environment, or life-style. The Wisconsin bill would prevent schools from requiring students to participate in role playing, and bar the use of children in any research project that inquires into the emotional or psychological characteristics of the pupils and their family.

The Wisconsin Education Association (WEA) vigorously attacked the bill, using a frequent—but surely irrelevant—argument: The bill is favored by "right wing organizations, fundamentalist religious groups, anti-sex education leaders." But Jil Wilson of the Wisconsin Federation of Teachers, a competing professional organization that supported the bill, wonders why WEA is so afraid of informing parents about what is happening in the schools. "Why do you object to or fear 'informed' parents? What are you doing?"[7]

The Hatch Amendment to the Elementary and Secondary Education Act, adopted in November of 1978, was also aimed at values clarification and other educational techniques designed by behavioral social scientists. The very proposal was a sign, according to columnist James J. Kilpatrick, "of the weird goings-on in public education." The purpose was to "crack down on the arrogant curiosity of a gaggle of crackpot psychologists who have invaded our schools," Kilpatrick said.[8]

The Hatch Amendment said: "No student shall be required, as part of any applicable program, to submit to psychiatric examination, testing, or treatment, or psychological examination, testing, or treatment, without the prior consent of the parent."

In Orrin Hatch's (R-Utah) comments to the Senate, he noted several offensive examples, including a Wisconsin program in sex education that starts at the kindergarten level. In this program ten year olds are told how to get an abortion. James Kilpatrick cited his own illustrations, including a questionnaire from California that asks fifth-grade boys, "Do you often play

with your penis?'' and girls, ''Do you often see your father with
no clothes on?'' In supporting the Hatch proposal, Senator S. I.
Hayakawa (R-Calif.) challenged the underlying assumptions of
these invasions of privacy:

> Everyone, it is believed, is to some extent neur-
> otic because of repression, inhibition, reaction
> formation, symbolic displacement, or what-
> ever. Everyone, therefore, needs diagnosis, to
> examine the extent and seriousness of his or her
> illness. Everyone, it hardly needs to be said,
> needs to be straightened out.[9]

Assisting students in identifying their values is important,
even crucial, in our day. However, the use of such techniques
with young children, who are easily manipulated by projective
techniques and have no frame of reference from which to
develop values, seems inappropriate at best. I doubt that such
programs are really neutral, especially when one considers the
reasons Paul Haubner, specialist for the National Education
Association (NEA), gives for resisting values parents would like
to see included in education. ''Our goals are incompatible with
theirs [parents]. . . . They want to tell you what the truth is and
not search for it. We must challenge values. The schools have to
have controversy.''[10]

LOOKING ''EAST'' FOR ANSWERS?

It is not that the schools aren't sometimes looking for
answers, it is just that they seem to find them in the strangest
places. Frances Adeney, research director for Spiritual
Counterfeits Project, studied the methods and ideologies in
some public schools; these methods seem to be rooted in world
views alien to traditional western philosophy.[11] For instance, she
cites a program made available from the Specially Funded Projects Office of the Los Angeles Public Schools called ''confluent
education,'' developed under the direction of Dr. Beverly
Gaylean. Here is an example of a first-grade class session of this
program, a meditative journey for children who are lying mo-
tionless in the room. The teacher recites:

> Relax and breathe deeply. Imagine your body

filling with sunlight. Bring the sun down, down
through the top of your head. Let pure light fill
your chest.

Bring the light down into your tummy, your
legs. This is the purest light, the light of the
universe. It is your light. Fill yourself with it.

Now imagine yourself being perfect. . . . Fill
yourself with the knowledge of being perfect.
This is your light, your intelligence, your sun.

You now contain all the light of the universe.
With that light within, you are at peace. You
are perfect. . . . You are intelligent, magnifi-
cent; you contain all of the wisdom of the
universe within yourself.[12]

Such an approach, Adeney notes, is "linked inextricably to
a set of religious assumptions." Dr. Gaylean herself attributes
the success of the system to the implied beliefs that we are not individuals but part of a universal consciousness—God or
spirit—which manifests itself in our material world. This universal consciousness is love, which each child can contain in his or
her "higher self" as the child gains counsel from the "spirit
guides" to tap into the universal mind.

Adeney quotes Gaylean as she states her own beliefs:

Once we begin to see that we are all God, that
we all have the attributes of God, I think the
whole purpose of human life is to reown the
Godlikeness within us; the perfect love, the
perfect wisdom, the perfect understanding, the
perfect intelligence, and when we do that, we
create back to that old, that essential oneness
which is consciousness. So my whole view is
very much based on that idea.

Adeney claims that schools are ripe for such "ex-
periments," since they are a "spiritual vacuum."[13]

Other sources also have unique solutions for our schools,
ones loaded with religious assumptions. In 1982 the Education
Network of the Association for Humanistic Psychology suggested that teachers incorporate a variety of new techniques into

education: the practices of doing yoga exercises, interpreting astrological charts, sending ESP messages, speaking with the "Higher Self," receiving messages from personal guides, and merging the mind into the collective consciousness.

Interestingly, Adeney warns Christians that the reintroduction of prayers into schools may result in forms of prayers quite hostile to Christianity. Because a prayer amendment could not limit the worship activities to certain beliefs, Christians could not complain about introducing students to "spirit guides" and eastern meditation.

SEX EDUCATION

Sex instruction in the schools has become a national debate. Many would have us believe the argument is between archaic religious fundamentalists and more modern doctors and educators. But the sides are not so clearly drawn. In 1980 the *Los Angeles Times* said a new sex education guide for teachers in California could have come from the presses of *Playboy,* for all the furor it provoked. In that state parents and community representatives have the right to review school materials. Here is a sample of some of the suggestions parents found in this particular teacher's manual:

●Beginning at age 3, youngsters might be taken on a tour of boys' and girls' bathrooms, with the teacher discussing the urinal as a topic of sex differences.

●At 9, pupils may begin to study menstruation, conception, ejaculation and nocturnal emissions and read booklets that say masturbation is acceptable and normal.

●To ages 9 to 11, a teacher might say, in a discussion of family problems, "Sometimes grandfather is fine; at other times he takes off his clothes, defecates on the floor . . . What are you going to do with grandfather?"

●Teachers may lead students 12 to 15 years old to "a local drug store and check the availability of contraceptive products."

●The youngsters might also be told, "If an adolescent really feels OK about having sex, then advance planning should not be a major problem.''

● It is also suggested that students might consider a wide variety of life-styles, including homosexuality, communes, group marriage and couples living together without marriage.[14]

Such programs are not limited to California. One authority described a Kansas sex education program as offering so many diverse sexual mores that children were romping freely through moral supermarkets.

The Kansas program utilized a text *Marriage and Family Today*, which is described in the publisher's catalog as having a "non-sexist, non-moralizing tone." It discusses various forms of behavior in and out of marriage, including "intimate friendship," which is defined by sexologist James Ramsey as an "otherwise traditional friendship in which sexual intimacy is considered appropriate behavior." Ramsey's views that "research" indicates that married persons need not hide these "intimate friendships" from their spouses is also noted. Onalee McGraw of The Heritage Foundation notes how this alleged "value free" sex education curriculum redefines morality. Adultery is now an "intimate friendship."[15] So slippery are such concepts that McGraw warns parents to be "constantly vigilant" about the introduction of courses from what she calls the "soft" social sciences: futurism, family studies, human relations, and humanistic psychology.

One sex education film was said to be "an X-rated real shocker!" You would think these words described an adult movie. But the *National Review* evaluated a sex education film for children with these explicit adjectives. C. Donald Cole, radio pastor of Moody Bible Institute, also spoke against the film, which was used in a suburban Chicago community in 1977. According to *National Review*, the film, *About Sex*, portrays "every kind of sexual relationship, normal or perverted, complete with gutter talk, back alley language, nudity, crudity, the whole bit. . . ." Frances Frech (writing in *The National Right to Life News*) lays the blame for this focus on sexuality squarely at the foot of Planned Parenthood, the film's sponsor. He calls the organization the "Sacred Cow" whose "milk is poisonous, bitter, as unhealthy and addictive as any drug." Yet, Frech notes, we allow our children to be fed on a diet of it.

Another sex education program—this time in Richmond, Virginia—involved a role reversal game called "Trade-off" where boys visited a Planned Parenthood Clinic for a pelvic examination, placing their feet in stirrups while girls walked in and out of the room. And in Ferndale, California, a high school sex education guide suggested boy-girl couples collaborate on worksheets to define *foreplay, erection,* and *ejaculation.*

Few aspects of public school education intrude into family rights as extensively as sex education, and as you have seen, the subject is often approached not only without values but with the implicit rejection of Christian perspectives. Do such programs really contribute to a child's education? Many who once advocated these programs are not at all sure. Dr. John Meeks of the Child and Adolescent Services of the Psychiatric Institute in Washington calls mandatory sex education programs "unwarranted and potentially destructive."[16]

Dr. Val Davajan, assistant professor and head physician at the University of California at Los Angeles, said in 1969, "I am convinced that those who have planned and are presently promoting this national sex education program have a very definite goal . . . to degrade and denigrate the mentality of an entire generation of American children."[17]

Another authority who is warning teachers and school administrators about the insidious effect of sex education is Dr. Louise Eickhoff, a British adult and child psychiatrist: "I first began to notice the correlation between these disturbed children and the fact that they had all been exposed to early compulsory sex education in schools after the last war. . . . We are not educating our children. We are corrupting them. . . ." She referred to hundreds of cases in her files that show the often serious emotional harm to children exposed to school sex programs.

Finally Dr. Rhoda L. Lorand, a practicing psychotherapist in New York City, linked the startling rise in venereal disease (VD) in the United States to the introduction of sex education in 1964, the year the Swedish program was imported into our country by Planned Parenthood, HEW, the Ford Foundation, and others. Lorand suggests that one of these groups should have noted that in that very same year Swedish authorities panicked at the results of ten years of their sex programs. One-hundred-forty physicians and two-hundred-thousand Swedes signed a plea that went to the minister of education; the petition deplored the obsession with sex exhibited by young people and noted that children had misunderstood instruction in sexual matters for encouragement to practice. The physicians observed that "the concept of love by young people has been reduced to sex," and that "their view of woman, marriage and the home is debased and virtues such as self-discipline, generosity, responsibility, idealism and personal fellowship are shunted aside. . . ."

Dr. Lorand points to a steady climb of VD in Sweden, beginning in 1954 when their sex instruction became mandatory. The current rise in VD in the United States parallels this phenomenon, she suggests.[18]

PARENTS ARE OFTEN RIGHT

Some researchers offer support for irate parents' complaints that textbooks are hostile to their values. A study by Donald Oppewal, a professor at Calvin College, reviewed two junior high literature anthologies that were published by the same company twenty-five years apart. The contemporary anthology contained one third as many references to theistic thought and practices as did the earlier edition.[19]

Harold Pflug studied Missouri textbooks and concluded that "the closer we get in textbook descriptions of present day life and literature, the fewer the theistic references. . . . There is a noticeable tapering off of religious references. . . . Thus an alert student may feel that the textbook dealing with today's problems no longer cites religion as a molding force in society."[20]

In Kanawha County, West Virginia, parents who were pictured by newspaper and media reporters as irrational, fundamentalist censors received support for their complaints from a study conducted by George Hillocks, a University of Chicago professor of education. After reviewing the language arts textbooks that precipitated this controversy, Hillocks noted that only six of the thirty-eight poems in these books dealt with any element in the Christian tradition. All six were "pejorative of Christianity, either directly in adverse comments about the shortcomings of Christianity or indirectly by showing Christians as hypocrites or fools."[21]

It's no wonder parents are upset. They "have a right to expect that the schools, in their teaching approaches and selection of instructional materials, will support the values and standards that their children are taught at home," said Terrell Bell, United States commissioner of education in 1974 and now secretary to the Department of Education. "And if the schools cannot support those values they must at least avoid deliberate destruction of them."[22]

Parents are not "censors" for expressing their concerns about the literature used in public schools. Yet whenever parents and local groups show such concern, they are pilloried as reactionaries. Judith Krug, director of the American Library Association's Office of Intellectual Freedom, has declared that the challenge to school books poses "the most strenuous attack . . . since the McCarthy era" to intellectual freedom.

Yet, as *Education Update* pointed out in July of 1982, these "liberals" consistantly apply a double standard—carefully seeking to root out racial or sexual discrimination or innuendo in school literature, but being outraged at concerns by parents about other moral issues. As *Education Update* put it: "In short, 'censors' are people whose politics and values differ from Krug's."

And who complained of censorship when New York City rejected a science text, *Life Science,* published by Prentice Hall, because it did not exclusively teach evolution?

Teachers and educational authorities aren't the only ones with a right to participate in evaluating literature, and their ideas are not the only ones worthy of consideration. As Scott Thomson, executive director of the National Association of Secondary School Principals, observed, "Most citizens simply do not accept the infallibility of teachers on matters of morality or values."[23] In fact, Professor Allan Glatthorn in *Dealing with Censorship* acknowledges the tendency of teachers to impose a bias:

> . . . We as English teachers need to show more acceptance and respect for values other than our own. Most of us are intellectuals who see ourselves as liberated; but too often such intellectual independence becomes distorted into a smug conviction that the traditional values of church, country, and family are childish abera-

tions that must be corrected. So we set about to
indoctrinate with our own brand of humanistic
relativism.[24]

Parents do have a right to fight such indoctrination. They
have a right to do more than just teach Christian morality in
their homes; they have a right to voice their concern about the
lack of morality in education at a time when there is a moral
vacuum in society.

Parents can fight back. Parents in River Forest, Illinois,
sued the state superintendent of public schools in 1980, and they
won a ruling that abstinence would be taught as another means
of preventing pregnancy. In the same year a New Jersey Coalition of Concerned Parents forced the state to raise the mandatory age for sex education from kindergarten to the sixth
grade.

LEGISLATION

State legislators are also beginning to listen to parents. The
Oklahoma State Senate and House recently approved a resolution that urged the state Textbook Committee to approve textbooks with content that "can be instrumental in guiding
children toward productive, law-abiding and meaningful lives."

Curriculum, the resolution said, should emphasize the
following:

● the importance of the family as the core of
American society
● should not degrade traditional roles of
men and women, boys and girls
● should show an awareness of the religious
and classical culture of the Western world
● should treat subjects of historical origins
of humankind in objective and unbiased manner.

Weldon David, president of the Oklahoma Education
Association, charged that the resolution is "a brand of indoctrination." But Senator Norman Lamb, a sponsor of the bill,
said the resolution shows the "will of the Oklahoma
Legislature" that textbooks reflect Christian values.[25]

The current deep fear of re-introducing "religious values" into the school through one-minute prayer is ironic beside the explosion of exotic, value-loaded curricula in other areas! We are "generating a population who are masters of sex, celibates of prayer," charged Michael Novak in an article in the *National Review*.

Obviously the prayer question is not the only issue that raises concern about the absence of Christian and moral values in the schools.

4

Black Monday

"**S**upreme Court outlaws official school prayers" screamed a *New York Times* banner headline on June 25, 1962. Bill Bright of Campus Crusade for Christ would later describe that day as "the darkest hour of the nation."

Even Paul Blanshard, a vigorous opponent of school prayer, called the 6-1 decision of the Supreme Court a "bombshell."[1] Indeed few Court decisions have set off such fireworks, blasts that have continued to explode for twenty years.

THE CULPRIT CASE

Though the decision was rendered in 1962, the case, *Engel* v. *Vitale,* began in 1958. And the prayer that was at issue was written seven years before that.

Someone once described a camel as "a horse put together by a committee." Apparently committee-written prayers are not any more graceful. In 1951 the New York State Board of Regents, a government body equivalent to a state board of education, produced a twenty-two word prayer for optional use by schools within the state. It wasn't much as prayers go. One commentator described the prayer as "more doctrinally flavorless than grace before a community chest luncheon."[2]

What do you think of this prayer?

Almighty God, we acknowledge our dependence upon Thee, and we beg Thy blessings

40

upon us, our parents, our teachers, and our
country.

It's certainly hard to imagine fighting over it. Surely the
prayer's fame has come from its rejection—not from its prophetic power. In 1952, *Christian Century* magazine said the prayer
was "likely to deteriorate quickly into an empty formality with
little, if any, spiritual significance."[3] A Lutheran church in
Peekskill, New York, found the prayer highly objectionable,
charging that Christ's name was "deliberately . . . omitted to
mollify non-Christian beliefs." Thus the words were a denial of
Christ. "Not a prayer but an abomination and a blasphemy."[4]

The New York City Board of Education chose not to utilize
the prayer, though the board did suggest the use of the fourth
stanza of the hymn "America," which declares:

> Our fathers' God, to thee,
> Author of liberty,
>   to Thee we sing
> Long may our land be bright
> With freedom's holy light;
> Protect us by thy might,
>   Great God, our King.

In fact, only as few as 10 percent of the school districts of
New York implemented the Regents' twenty-two word invocation as part of their morning exercises. One district that did,
however, was the Union Free District No. 9 in New Hyde Park,
New York, a suburb of New York City.

For some time the district had expressed concern about the
moral character of education. In 1956 the school board had
voted 6-1 to put copies of the Ten Commandments in all the
classrooms, but the state education commissioner banned them
because they would lead to controversy. The Brooklyn *Tablet*
responded by calling for his resignation.[5]

When the district finally adopted the Regents' Prayer,
Lawrence Roth, a resident, placed an ad in a local paper asking
for taxpaying parents who wished to join him in challenging the
practice. One couple who took up the cause were Steven I. Engel
and his wife, whose children attended school in the district.
Altogether five sets of parents objected to the school board's

policy: two were Jewish, one a member of the Ethical Culture Society, one a Unitarian, and one a nonbeliever. The plaintiffs were represented by William Butler, an attorney for the American Civil Liberties Union, and a suit was filed against the school district, *Engel* v. *Vitale* (William J. Vitale, Jr., was president of the New Hyde Park School Board). The suit alleged that the practice of opening the school day with the Regents' Prayer was unconstitutional. The use of a state-written prayer violated the prohibition against the establishment of religion in the First Amendment and therefore violated the plaintiff's rights.

Public reaction to the Vitales, the Roths (who had run the ad), and other plaintiffs was largely negative. A local paper simply asked, "How crazy can you get?" A stream of propaganda, calls, and mail—saying "Wipe the smiles off your atheistic faces" and "Haven't they run you out of town yet, Commie, Jew Rat,"—was directed against Roth.

The state courts upheld the school district, directing the district to assure that students were not compelled to participate; and the district obligingly allowed students to be excused.

Then an appeal was made to the United States Supreme Court. Before the appeal was heard, seventeen state attorneys general filed briefs in support of school prayer.

On April 3, 1962, the case was argued. On June 25, the final day of the term, the Court delivered its 6-1 decision, with only Justice Potter Stewart dissenting. (Two justices did not participate in the decision.)

The Court's decision in this case—and other prayer and religion cases—is based on the sixteen words in the Religion Clause of the First Amendment.

THOSE CRUCIAL SIXTEEN WORDS

The Religion Clause contains two separate prohibitions on government:

> (1) Congress shall make no law respecting an establishment of religion . . .
>
> (2) . . . or prohibiting the free exercise thereof.

The first of these two prohibitions is referred to as the Establishment Clause, the second as the Free Exercise Clause. The reader unfamiliar with American legal history should note that the prohibitions initially related to Congress, not to the states. The First Amendment prohibits the national government, not the state government, from passing laws respecting an establishment of religion or prohibiting the free exercise thereof. Later court decisions have extended these prohibitions to the states.

Some reviewers of the language and debates of the Constitutional convention have noted that the wording does not prohibit *the* establishment of religion, but *an* establishment of religion. This wording was deliberate, says Michael Malbin in his book, *Religion and Politics.* The colonists intended to outlaw official activities that promoted one sect over another. It was not a prohibition of favoritism toward religion itself.

THE MAJORITY OPINION

The Supreme Court's majority opinion, which was written by Justice Hugo Black, declared that the practice of reciting the Regents' Prayer was indeed "wholly inconsistent" with the constitutional prohibition against the establishment of religion. The court noted that the daily "invocation of God's blessings" is quite clearly a "religious activity." It is "a solemn avowal of divine faith."

Black particularly noted the impermissibility of the state's involvement in writing prayers, and agreed with the appellants that the use of such state prayers "breaches the constitutional wall of separation." The constitutional prohibition against the establishment of religion "must at least mean that in this country it is no part of the business of government to compose official prayers for any group of the American people to recite as part of a religious program carried on by the government."

Black rejected the claims of the school board that the nondenominational character of the prayer and the voluntariness of participation saved it from constitutional challenge. Under the Establishment Clause, a violation "does not depend upon any showing of direct governmental compulsion," Black insisted.

The Court also rejected the claim that it was being hostile to religion and to prayer by striking this prayer down. "Nothing, of course, could be more wrong. . . . The history of man is inseparable from the history of religion. Religious convictions and commitments to the power of prayer caused men to come to this country, filled with the hope that they could pray when they pleased to the God of their faith." These men of prayer, who fought for the adoption of the Constitution and Bill of Rights, knew that to "put an end to government control of religion and of prayer was not . . . to destroy either." Indeed, Black insisted, "It is neither sacrilegious nor antireligious to say that each separate government in this country should stay out of the business of writing or sanctioning official prayers."

The majority opinion acknowledged that the prayer in question was brief, and perhaps of seeming little threat to the establishment of religion, but Black quoted the words of James Madison: "It is proper to take alarm at the first experiment on our liberties."

ONE DISSENT

"I think the decision is wrong," declared the only dissenting justice, Potter Stewart. He insisted that the majority had misconstrued the constitutional principle of establishment; allowing schoolchildren to say a prayer is not the establishment of an official religion. But refusing such a right denies these children "the opportunity of sharing in the spiritual heritage of our Nation." The state of New York had not established a religion anymore than the United States government had in imprinting "In God We Trust" on its coins or declaring in the Pledge of Allegiance that this nation is "under God," Stewart said. By these acts we recognize and follow "the deeply entrenched and highly cherished spiritual traditions of our Nation—traditions which come to us from those who almost two hundred years ago avowed their 'firm Reliance on the Protection of divine Providence' when they proclaimed the freedom and independence of this brave new world."

IS GOD UNCONSTITUTIONAL?

Sam Ervin, senator from North Carolina, immediately declared, "The Supreme Court has made God unconstitutional." Indeed, the reaction to the decision on "Black Monday" was vigorous. Newspaper headlines were followed by quotes from angry and concerned religious leaders, politicians, and a variety of citizen groups. As one observer noted, the debates "cannot be said to have been conducted in a spirit of Christian charity." If as much energy had gone into actual prayers in the schools, things might have been quite different.

While the religious community was rather significantly divided on the issue, wide attention was given to the reactions of critics. Episcopalian cleric James Pike declared the decision "threatens the public school idea itself" and "desecrates" both the schools and the nation. It was, he insisted, a new declaration of independence—"independence from God." For Pike, the attempt to create a neutrality in public education was impossible; a "Godless institution is no more neutral than a godly one."

The next day, Judge Ida May Adams of the Los Angeles Municipal Court opened court as usual, with prayer, but modified the content somewhat for the occasion:

> God bless the Supreme Court,
> And in Your wisdom let it be shown the error of
> its ways.[6]

Billy Graham called it "another step towards the secularization of the United States," and Cardinal Spellman said he was "shocked and frightened."[7] The Catholic bishop of Dallas-Fort Worth suggested that American public schools would have to "start bootlegging religion into the classrooms."[8] *America*, a Jesuit publication, called it "a decision that spits in the face of history."[9]

POLITICAL REACTIONS

Politicians joined the assault. Robert C. Byrd of West Virginia wondered, "Can it be that we, too, are ready to embrace the foul concept of atheism. . . . Somebody is tampering with America's soul."[10] Byrd's notion that the decision weakened our defense against Communist atheism has been a frequent charge. Professor Charles Rice noted, in a book highly critical of the Court, that the world struggle in which the United States is engaged has a spiritual dimension; our very effectiveness requires an affirmation that our rights are derived from God.[11]

More than one politician pointed out that on the same day that the Supreme Court banned prayers it affirmed the rights of publishers of homosexually oriented materials to use the United States mails, a result Representative August E. Johansen

(R-Mich.) described as "Obscenity, yes: prayer, no."[12]

The National Governor's Conference, which was in session, promptly and unanimously adopted a resolution (New York Governor Rockefeller abstaining) calling for a constitutional amendment.

Many American officials vowed to ignore the decision. "We will go on having Bible readings and prayers in the schools of this state as we always have," said North Carolina Governor Terry Sanford. A Long Island, New York, school superintendent said the Court's orders would be defied since "a school without a prayer is not a school."[13]

PUBLIC REACTION

The Court received over five-thousand letters on the *Engel* decision! And the government printing office said they had larger public demand for this court opinion than for any other they could remember. Some of the hostility was even directed at the whole integrity of the Court. Signs along highways in North Carolina that had called out Impeach Warren—Save America, now added a line: Save Prayer.

A few voices urged caution. After all, the Court had only ruled that the state should not be in the business of writing prayers. *Presbyterian Life* carried an editorial: "Keeping Our Shirt On." *Life* magazine, though warning the court not to aspire to becoming a "super school board" for the nation, called the decision a "sharp reminder to parents" that they can't give up their job of religious education to the public schools.[14]

The reactions of school boards were in the main more restrained. Some indicated an intent to comply. A few, however, tried imaginative antidotes like the Hicksville (Long Island) Board of Education, which approved the use of the fourth stanza of the "Star Spangled Banner" for an opening exercise:

> Then conquer we must
> When our cause it is just;
> And this be our motto:
> "In God is our trust."[15]

However, the New York commissioner of education held this practice impermissible.

In Levittown, New York, the schools tried the fourth verse

of the hymn "America," mentioned earlier: "Our father's God to Thee/Author of Liberty/to Thee we sing. . . ." But that, too, was struck down. And in Netcong, New Jersey, a voluntary plan to read the prayers of chaplains of the United States Senate and the House of Representatives was instituted—unsuccessfully.

Back in the New Hyde Park School District, the Roths and the other plaintiffs continued to be harrassed. When Mrs. Roth was asked to react to the attacks, she responded: "If their God teaches them to wish my kids get polio and my house be bombed, then I think He hasn't done a very good job."

5

The Supreme Court
Strikes Again

Educators and religious leaders who favored school prayer, shocked by their defeat in the *Engel* case, now clung desperately to one hope: that the repercussions of the Court's decision against the Regents' Prayer would be limited. It seemed that the Court had only struck down officially written and prescribed prayers. A spokesman for the Education Department of New Jersey went so far as to comment that the decision did not apply to his state, since no official prayers had been prepared by school authorities there.[1]

Sam Duker, writing in the *Education Forum* shortly after *Engel,* insisted, "It is extremely unlikely that school practices relating to non-sectarian prayers will be seriously affected." The *Engel* case was in one sense easy, a "clay pigeon," observed another law commentator. A few legal scholars even wondered why the Court had bothered to take *Engel* when there were other cases that focused on the more central question: Whether or not *any* school prayer or devotional exercises were permissible.

But the *Harvard Law Review*, among others, predicted the future accurately when it suggested that the Court was following a deliberate strategy by postponing other cases that dealt with Bible reading and the use of the Lord's Prayer—practices traditional in as many as 50 percent of the nation's schools.[2] The Court began with the Regents' Prayer to provide a little "judicial inoculation calculated to give the public partial immunity to the affliction which was to ensue,"[3] the law review prophesied.

And, indeed, it was right. Almost one year after *Engel*, on June 17, 1963, the Supreme Court issued two more controversial decisions on cases heard together: *Murray* v. *Curlett* and *Abingdon* v. *Schempp*.

Murray v. *Curlett*

The *Murray* case was from Baltimore, Maryland, where the Board of School Commissioners provided that there would be opening school exercises consisting of the "reading, without comment, of a chapter in the Holy Bible and/or the use of the Lord's Prayer." William J. Murray, a teenage student, and his mother, now the famed atheist Madalyn Murray O'Hair, complained about the morning exercises. In his new book, *My Life Without God*, William Murray tells how the case began one fall when his mother registered him late for school, because they had been out of the country, trying unsuccessfully to defect to Russia.

> We walked down the long hall in silence, following the signs pointing to the school office. The doors to the classrooms stood open. As we passed one class we saw the students standing with their hands over their hearts, reciting the Pledge of Allegiance to the flag. My mother's face reddened. "Do they do this every day, or is this something special?" she demanded.
>
> "Every day."
>
> She stopped dead in front of another open classroom door. Mother's eyes widened. The students were standing beside their desks with their heads bowed, reciting the Lord's Prayer. "Why in h— didn't you tell me about this?" she spat in a hoarse whisper.
>
> "We were on our way to the Soviet Union to become great commissars, remember?"
>
> "You smart aleck," she hissed, raising her hand menancingly. I ducked back to avoid the expected blow, but she changed her mind and just froze, a glare in her eyes. "You should have told me about this!"

I shrugged. I knew why I hadn't told her. Every time I mentioned anything about school, she found some reason to belittle or strike me. It seemed wise not to tell her the true reason now, though, since she was steaming with anger. Instead, I just drew a deep breath and walked on toward the office. She strode along behind, her stocky body now tense and ready for battle.

In moments we found the counselor's office, and as we entered, a young, slender man looked at us expectantly. "Hello, may I help you?" he asked pleasantly.

"You sure can, but first I want to know why those kids are praying?" Mother shouted, advancing to within inches of his desk. "Why are they doing that? It's un-American and unconstitutional!"

The man swallowed. "I, uhh, well . . . Is your son a student here?" he asked.

"No," she answered. "But he will be starting today. I'm an atheist, and I don't want him taught any g—d— prayers."

"Look, Mrs.—uhh, what is your name?"

"Murray—Madalyn Murray."

"Look, Mrs. Murray, nobody's ever complained about this before that I know of." He paused, searching for more ammunition. "Besides, even those who aren't very religious still think this sort of thing helps improve the tone of the school day. . . ."

"Nonsense! That's just a bunch of g—d— nonsense, and you know it!"

"Hey, I don't want to fight with you about this. Nothing you or I do here this morning is going to change anything. Besides, let me tell you this. There were prayers in the schools of this city before there was a United States of America. If our forefathers wanted us to stop the practice, they would have told us that when they formed the government. Now, shall we enroll your son?''

Mother was so furious she had nearly turned purple. The counselor filled in the late enrollment forms for her to sign. When he was finished, he drew a large ''T'' on the label of my file. I learned later it stood for ''troublemaker.''

Mother aimed one last verbal shot at him. ''This won't be the last time you hear from me about your g—d— prayers in this school!''

''Madam,'' he replied, ''I don't have to take this! If you don't like what we do here, put your son in a private school.''

''It doesn't matter where I put him. You people have to be stopped,'' she replied.

''Then why don't you sue us?'' he asked.

Mother stared at him, then motioned for me to leave. Unknowingly, the counselor had given Mother what would turn out to be a very devastating idea. She certainly would sue.[4]

William Murray was encouraged by his mother to participate in ''civil disobedience in a challenge of the constitutionality of religious ceremonies in public schools.'' Young Bill went on an eighteen-day strike at Woodbourne Junior High School, refusing to obey the compulsory attendance laws. It was not an easy route for the boy. When he returned to school, he was ostracized, and reportedly beaten up.

But the national attention given to the strike forced the Maryland legislature to provide for the excusal of objecting students. Still the Murrays filed a lawsuit, alleging that the practice subjected an atheist's ''freedom of conscience to the rule of the majority.'' The practice, they said, resulted in their beliefs being rendered ''sinister, alien and suspect'' in the eyes of their friends and neighbors.

John Curtlett, president of the Board of School Commissioners of Baltimore City, successfully had the case dismissed by the trial court, and a Maryland court of appeals upheld this dismissal in a 4-3 decision. The court of appeals took special note that no student was compelled to participate, and thus constitutional rights were not infringed upon. Now the Murrays appealed to the United States Supreme Court, which agreed to review the case. The outcome became history.

Abington v. Schempp

The *Schempp* case came from Philadelphia, where Mr. and Mrs. Edward Schempp had three children in local schools: Ellroy, a senior; Roger, an eighth grader; and Donna Kay, a seventh grader. As Unitarians, they took exception to the Pennsylvania law that required: "at least ten verses from the Holy Bible shall be read, without comment, at the opening of each public school on each school day." The law provided that any teacher who did not conduct the exercises was subject to discharge. Ellroy, a senior in high school, sought permission to be excused, but the assistant principal advised him to remain in the classroom. Later the assistant principal testified that requiring Ellroy to remain in the room taught pupils "to show respect"; "matters of conscience and religion were not as important here as merely conforming to the school rule," he said.[5]

The Schempps filed suit in a federal district court, seeking to have the enforcement of the statute forbidden, because it violated their rights. The district court agreed, and struck down the statute as unconstitutional. As the state of Pennsylvania appealed to the Supreme Court, the Pennsylvania General Assembly amended the school code so that any student could be excused upon written request of the parents. In the light of this change, the Supreme Court sent the case back to the district court for reconsideration. Again, the district court held the statute unconstitutional. Again the state and the school board appealed to the United States Supreme Court.

THE SETTING FOR
SUPREME COURT REVIEW

In many ways the two cases promised to have a far broader impact than the *Engel* case, because many school districts across the country had devotional exercises of one form or another. A 1946 survey had shown that twenty-four states permitted such devotional exercises; later, in 1961, one survey showed that 41 percent of the school districts read the Bible and about half of the school districts had some kind of devotional exercise. Twelve states and the District of Columbia *required* Bible reading—providing that the teacher did not comment on the readings. Most school boards allowed students whose parents did not wish their children to participate to be excused or to leave the classroom.[6]

Murray and Schempp were not the first challenges to school Bible reading. In Cincinnati in 1869, Catholics had objected to school Bible readings, complaining that "reading without note or comment . . . is likely to lead to the adoption of dangerous error." The complaints led to a suit, John D. Minor, et al. v. Board of Education of the City of Cincinnati. The court upheld the right of the school district to make decisions about prayer and Bible reading in the city's schools. In this case, the school board chose to stop Bible reading.

Disputes about Bible reading had also centered on the use of particular versions, with Catholics frequently objecting to the prescribed use of the King James Version. The issue even led to riots and killings in Philadelphia as early as 1844. But the cases now before the Court were national in scope and were not raising questions about doctrine or versions, but about the constitutionality of the whole practice.

THE DECISIONS

On June 17, 1963, the Court again struck out at religious practice in public education, a decision Senator Strom Thurmond described as "another major triumph for the forces of secularism and atheism."

Justice Tom Clark noted in the majority opinion that indeed religion had been closely identified with our American history and government; the history of man is inseparable from religion. Clark (quoting Justice Douglas in Zorach v. Clauson) acknowledged that "we are a religious people whose institutions presuppose the existence of a Supreme Being," and that the founding fathers believed devotedly in a Supreme Being in whom the rights of man were rooted. These traditions, Clark observed, continue to be evidenced in the prayers in courtrooms, in oaths of office, and in the existence of military chaplaincies.

However, Clark declared that this religious commitment does not preclude an equal commitment to religious liberty, a liberty our founders advocated because of their own painful experiences of religious intolerance. This liberty, Clark declared, is essential in a country as diverse as our own.

Then Justice Clark moved to the heart of the majority's

argument: the necessity of governmental neutrality toward religion. The Court quoted Judge Alphonso Taft in an earlier case: "The government is neutral, and, while protecting all, it prefers none, and it disparages none."

The Court "unequivocally" rejected the argument of some that the First Amendment only forbids governmental preference of one religion over another. Rather, the First Amendment "uproots" all support of religion by government. The purpose of the establishment prohibition is "to create a complete and permanent separation of the spheres of religious activity and civil authority."

The neutrality must extend to public education, Clark held. Constitutional policy does not deny the value or necessity of religious training and observance—indeed it secures their free exercise. But it does "deny that the state can undertake or sustain" it. In fact, the very union of government and religion tends to "destroy government and degrade religion."

Clark then established two parts of the tripartite test to determine whether a given government act constituted an impermissible establishment of religion. These two prongs (along with the third prong added in later cases) have become the critical instrument for Court analysis of establishment claims. In the words of the Court:

> The test may be stated as follows: what are the
> purpose and the primary effect of the enact-
> ment? If either is the advancement or inhibition
> of religion, then the enactment exceeds the
> scope of legislative power as circumscribed by
> the Constitution. . . . There must be a secular
> legislative purpose and a primary effect that
> neither advances nor inhibits religion.

Applying this *purpose* and *effect* test, the Court held that such school exercises are impermissible. They are religious exercises and are mandatory parts of the school curriculum, which are imposed on students required by law to attend school, held in school buildings, and utilize teachers employed by the state; therefore, they violate the Establishment Clause.

The Court thus found that there was an impermissible religious purpose. It rejected the schools' claims that the secular purposes—promoting moral values, contradicting the materialistic trends in society, and the teaching of literature—were sufficient to preserve the practices. The fact that students were allowed to excuse themselves did not change the character of these religious acts as required components of the schools' programs, and thus it was no defense.

The Court rejected two common arguments for including religious exercises in schools. First, the Court specifically rejected the claim that its decision contributed to a "religion of secularism." The state should not establish a secularist religion by showing active hostility to religion or affirmatively opposing it, the Court acknowledged. But this decision does not do that, Clark insisted. He noted that "it may well be said that one's education is not complete without a study of comparative religion and its relationship to the advancement of civilization." Clark further noted that the Bible is worthy of study; its objective study may be a part of an educational program.

Second, the Court dealt with the claim that the students' rights of free exercise of religion were being denied. The majority's right to free exercise of religion was not infringed by removing the state from the conduct of these religious exercises, Clark argued. The majority does not have a constitutional right to "use the machinery of the state to practice its belief."

Clark concluded his opinion by citing the "exalted" place of religion in our society, one achieved by a "long tradition of reliance on the home, the church and the inviolable citadel of the individual heart and mind." It is not within the power of the state to invade that citadel, whether to aid or oppose religion. "In the relationship between man and religion, the State is firmly committed to a position of neutrality."

Concurring opinions were also written by Justice William Douglas and Justice William Brennan. Justice Brennan's opinion, unlike Douglas's, was quite lengthy, more than twice as long as Clark's majority opinion. A number of Brennan's observations are of special interest. He acknowledged that constitutional prohibitions meet their "severest test" in the public education arena, because it is such a vital institution associated with the preservation of our values.

Brennan reviewed the shift in education since the days of the founding fathers—from a primarily private, religious activity to an activity of the government. We are also a much more diverse nation today, he noted, no longer divided merely between differing Protestant sects. Because of this, "practices which may have been objectionable to no one in the time of Jefferson and Madison may today be highly offensive . . ."

Brennan further argued that public schools, unlike parochial schools, are supported by public funds; their function is the training of children in an atmosphere "free of parochial, divisive or separatist influences. . . ." It is a patriotic heritage, not a theistic or atheistic heritage, which the public schools teach. The Constitution protects the rights of parents to choose an alternative education, a school that more accurately reflects the values and faith of their family.

ANOTHER DISSENT FROM STEWART

Justice Potter Stewart, who dissented in *Engel*, was again the sole dissenter. Stewart focused on the rights of parents who wanted their children to have the advantages of religious exercises, and he rejected Brennan's implication that the private school offered this option. Freedoms of religion are to be available to all persons, not just those who may be able to afford a private education for their children, he said.

The practices in Pennsylvania and Maryland are constitutional, according to Stewart, because of the need to provide free exercise for those who are in the context of a compulsory educational system, which substantially structures a child's life. "If religious exercises are held to be an impermissible activity in schools, religion is placed at an artificial and state-created disadvantage." Allowing these religious exercises is essential if the state is to be truly neutral; a refusal would constitute not neutrality, but the "establishment of a religion of secularism." The state must assure that pressure is not put on any child to participate in such exercises, but the state does not have to assure an atmosphere that keeps children "scrupulously insulated" from an awareness that there are differences in religious beliefs, or that some of their fellow students wish to pray.

Stewart did not see enough evidence in the records of these cases to determine whether or not the programs created impermissible pressure on students to participate. Therefore, he felt the cases ought to be remanded to the lower courts in order to determine the facts.

REACTIONS: ROUND TWO

Again the reaction to the Court's ruling was swift. Supporters of the decisions were called atheists, free thinkers, ultraliberals, a bunch of crackpots, and inverse bigots.[7]

Billy Graham called the decision "shocking." Other religious leaders expressed dismay, including Cardinal Cushing, who said it was a "great tragedy" that the greatest book ever written could not be read in schools. Bishop Fulton J. Sheen observed, "Our schools are now officially put on the same level as the Communist schools."[8] The same note was echoed by Cardinal McIntyre of Los Angeles who said that it meant the abandonment of our American heritage of philosophy, religion, and freedom "in imitation of Soviet philosophy."[9] Robert Cooke of the National Association of Evangelicals called the decision a "sad departure from the nation's heritage under God."

Other religious groups defended the decision. In June of 1963, the General Board of the National Council of Churches declared that "neither true religion nor good education is dependent upon the devotional use of the Bible in public school programs." Perhaps in anticipation of the Supreme Court's decision, the 175th General Assembly of the United Presbyterian Church declared in May of 1963 that devotional Bible reading and prayers "tend toward indoctrination or meaningless ritual" and should be omitted.[10]

POLITICAL REACTIONS

"Despite the Supreme Court ruling, I am urging school teachers and schools to continue the reading of the Bible and to continue praying in classrooms," declared Senator Olin Johnson of South Carolina. He reminded school authorities that there were no penalties for such action until a court injunction was obtained "in each individual and every case."[11] The reactions of politicians and school officials often evidenced little intent to follow the decision. South Carolina Attorney General Daniel McLeod said, "We are not much concerned about what the Supreme Court has ruled."[12]

And on the very day of the ruling, the superintendent of education in South Carolina said his state would ignore the decision. North Carolina, Alabama, and Mississippi soon agreed. Massachusetts immediately cancelled scheduled prayers at their graduation exercises, but their response was an exception.

Even some courts were resistant. When a case (*Chamberlin v. Dade County Board of Public Instruction*) was remanded to the Supreme Court of Florida for review in the light of *Schempp*, the court reheard the case, but still refused to order the discontinuance of Bible reading and the Lord's Prayer. If these practices were to be denied to the children of Florida, it would have to be done by the Supreme Court of the United States, not by a Florida Court.[13]

Less than a year later, a *U.S. News and World Report* survey found that fifteen states had refused to give up their devotional exercises. Some officials had reacted like the attorney general of Delaware, who advised schools to continue to obey the state law, which required the daily reading of five verses of the Bible and the recitation of the Lord's Prayer. A study five years after the decision still noted substantial noncompliance by school districts.[14]

Editorial comment was more restrained, but David Lawrence of *U.S. News and World Report* seemed to reverse course from his support of *Engel*. Now Lawrence declared that "plainly, a constitutional amendment has become absolutely necessary."[15]

In addition to the popular outrage, a number of surprising voices were raised against the decision. Dean Erwin Griswold of Harvard Law School wondered if in our country of great tolerance, it isn't important also that "the minorities who have benefited so greatly from that toleration be tolerant too."[16] And noted historian Sidney Hook said the decision was "perverse," reaching a "new low, not only in argument but in the improvisation of fact," interfering with the local processes of accommodation and compromise.

CONGRESSIONAL RESPONSES

Neither was the reaction among the politicians all talk. Way back when the Congress had convened the morning after *Engel*, the constitutional amendment bandwagon had begun. A total of 147 amendments to reverse *Engel* had been submitted in the next weeks, involving over 75 senators and representatives.

The Becker Amendment

The amendment proposal of Congressman Becker finally had become the focus of House congressional action. The

Becker Amendment provided that:

> Section 1. Nothing in this Constitution shall be deemed to prohibit the offering, reading from, or listening to prayers or biblical scriptures, if participation therein is on a voluntary basis, in any governmental or public school, institution or place.
> Section 2. Nothing in this Constitution shall be deemed to prohibit making reference to belief in, reliance upon, or invoking the aid of God or a Supreme Being in any governmental or public document, proceeding, activity, ceremony, school, institution or place, or upon any coinage, currency, or obligation of the United States.
> Section 3. Nothing in this article shall constitute an establishment of religion.

Becker's amendment, like all the others, had been referred to the House Committee on the Judiciary, chaired by Representative Emmanuel Cellar, who was not at all sympathetic. He supported the Court's decision.[17] Cellar declined to hold hearings on the amendment, despite considerable pressure, and efforts to remove the bill from his committee fell short of the necessary two-thirds vote. All the amendments had died with Congress's adjournment on October 13, 1962. Similar efforts had been under way in the Senate, but those three amendment proposals also died in the Senate Committee on the Judiciary when the 87th Congress adjourned.

When the 88th Congress opened in January of 1963, new proposals had been introduced. In the House, major attention had again been drawn to the bill proposed by Representative Becker. Again his amendment had been referred to the Judiciary Committee chaired by Emmanuel Cellar, who scheduled no hearings.

It was not until the court handed down the *Schempp* and *Murray* decisions in June of 1963 that any movement toward hearings began in the House, and the hearings weren't held until April of 1964. They revealed wide support for the Court's decision, and a lack of support for a prayer amendment among religious leaders of major denominations and groups such as the National Council of Churches. Father Drinan, a Catholic activist, warned against "tampering with the venerated language of the Constitution," and the conservative magazine, *Christianity Today*, called the amendment proposal "dangerous" and "piecemeal" and concluded that "it did not merit support."[18] But the bill had considerable grass-roots support from the American people. Perhaps Carl McIntyre, a Presbyterian minister, summed it up best when he told Congress that if the people were the judges they "would today declare the Supreme Court's decision unconstitutional."[19]

Likewise there had been no action at all in the Senate until June 17, when the *Schempp* decision was handed down. Soon eight proposals were introduced, but the Senate took no action on them.

The Dirksen Amendment

In 1966 the issue again became a focus of national attention, under the tutelage of Republican Floor Leader Senator Everett Dirksen. Dirksen's bill did not seek to protect the sort of government involvement that was present in the *Engel* and *Abington* situations; rather it allowed schools to permit student-initiated prayers during a period set aside by the schools. The bill said that nothing in the Constitution prohibited the administrator of a school or building from "providing for or permitting the voluntary participation of students or others in prayer," though it did not authorize such officials to "prescribe the form or content" of any prayer. Again the bill was stalled in an unsympathetic Judiciary Committee until Dirksen successfully moved to substitute his bill for a minor bill under consideration on the Senate floor. On September 21, a majority (49-37) voted to send the amendment to the states, but this was short of the required two-thirds vote.

Wylie Amendment

In 1971 an amendment again was center stage, this time introduced by Representative Chalmers P. Wylie (R-Ohio). The amendment provided that:

> Nothing contained in this Constitution shall
> abridge the right of persons lawfully assembled,

in any public building which is supported in whole or in part through the expenditure of public funds, to participate in voluntary prayer or meditation. (Prior to a change in the wording it had read "nondenominational" rather than "voluntary.")

The bill was supported by intense lobbying efforts by grassroots citizens' groups. Again the House Judiciary Committee stalled the bill, and it didn't come to a vote on the floor of the House until a discharge petition removed it from committee and brought it to the floor for action. But when the Wylie proposals were put to a vote on November 8, the 240-162 vote in favor was still short of the required two-thirds vote. The matter deadended there until the recent efforts of Senator Helms and the newly proposed amendment by the president.

As in a fencing match, those on both sides of the prayer issue continue to parry and thrust, each defending their understanding of the Constitution's intent and their vision of America. In the midst of the fray, school prayers seem symbolic. To some they represent the best of our heritage. To others, they are obsolete traditions America should leave behind her.

6

Why Can't
Johnny Pray?

A "school prayer wart" was diagnosed by the *New York Times* in 1980, a wart that has been growing below—and on the surface—of our national consciousness for years. In fact, the issue has been a persistent irritation since 1962 and 1963 when the Supreme Court issued its controversial decisions against school prayer.

"Prayer is creeping back into public schools. . . . it seems to me they're trying it more and more,"[1] declared Professor Richard Dierenfield, chairman of the Department of Education at Macalester College in Minnesota. Those who seek to combat this "creeping" disease challenge offending schools in the nation's courts. But despite this pressure, some offenders stubbornly persist, and the battle is on. . . .

In Texas, the Aldine Independent School District and the ACLU are squaring off in court over the school's marching song, which includes a prayer: "Dear God, please bless our school and all it stands for. Help keep us free from sin, honest and true, with courage and faith to make our school the victor. In Jesus' name we pray."

"I'm surprised that twenty years after the major Supreme Court cases, there is still such a prayer," the ACLU attorney in the case commented.

The prayer wart is also found as far north as LaGrange, Ohio, where the principal of a local school recites the Lord's Prayer over the public address system. The response of those who are trying to inoculate our country against the disease:

"They can't do it!" ACLU Cleveland chapter director Eileen Roberts vehemently denounced the practice. Still the LaGrange Board of Education voted 3-2 to continue the morning devotion.

Some who nurture school prayers suffer for their persistence. Lloyd Fink, a teacher in Harrisburg, Pennsylvania, was recently fired for praying and reading Bible stories in his class. He appealed the dismissal, but a Pennsylvania Commonwealth court upheld the decision.

STATES SEEK SOLUTIONS

Some states have made efforts either to defy the Supreme Court rulings against prayer or to get around them. About a dozen states have enacted silent meditation statutes. In July of 1982, Alabama passed a law authorizing teachers to lead "willing students" in prayer and suggesting a state-written prayer as the New York regents did. As of this writing, court response is still pending.

Massachusetts and Louisiana recently enacted statutes that authorized forms of voluntary classroom prayer. But the courts persistently find such attempts unconstitutional.

The Massachusetts law, passed in 1979, stated that each school could allow a time for teachers to invite student volunteers to lead in prayer. The statute allowed any pupil who did not wish to participate to be excused.

Civil libertarians immediately protested the statute. Even before it took effect, some school administrators objected, foreseeing confusion. One teacher from Hollison, Massachusetts, predicted it would "create chaos . . . a nightmare." Some predicted filibusters and teachers refusing to cooperate.

The *National Review* spoofed the educators' fears in a sarcastic fictional report, "And It Came to Pass," on the first day of the law's operation:

> Sure enough, on the morning of February 3, the entire town of Holliston was swept away in a flood. An earthquake—rated 9.8 on the Richter scale—took hundreds of lives in the city of Belmont. An epidemic of cholera rages even now in Amherst. Flash fires have struck homes in Methuen, where prophets ranged in the streets. . . . The American Red Cross has been unable

> to find volunteers to enter the state. The
> American Civil Liberties Union has asked for
> emergency donations to finance the construc-
> tion of an ark. Meanwhile, civil liberties have
> been widely curtailed. Governor King has im-
> posed martial law, and has asked the state's
> citizens to refrain from acts of prayer and sup-
> plication until the crisis has passed.[2]

All kidding aside, during the statute's brief life, *Time* did
report these astonishing occurrences: A Plymouth sixth grader
prayed for the release of the hostages. A pupil in Scituate,
Massachusetts, prayed for a volleyball victory. Many students
chose to recite the Lord's Prayer. A few opted out. And a Jewish
girl said she couldn't pray because her prayers were in Hebrew
and she couldn't speak Hebrew.

It didn't take long for the Massachusetts statute to be
challenged, and in *Kent* v. *Commissioner of Education,* the
Massachusetts Supreme Court struck down the practice. The
court held that the primary effect of the law was to aid religion,
and that as such it was unconstitutional. The court rejected the
claim that the purpose was primarily to teach religious toleration
and awareness of religious viewpoints. The provision for excusal
for those not wishing to participate did not save the practice
from being essentially coercive, because it still relied upon the
power and prestige of government.

The court cited objectionable components of state involvement: "sponsored and put into effect by state and local
officials"; "conducted from day to day by teachers employed as
public employees"; "carried out on public property, during
school time and as part of the school exercises." It is not, the
court declared, "unreasonable" to require students to keep their
religious practices outside the classroom. This does not deny
them their rights to the free exercise of religion.

The state of Louisiana also passed a statute that permitted
local districts to develop a policy allowing five minutes of voluntary prayer in the classrooms at the beginning of the school day.

The statute (Section 2115[B] of Title 17, Louisiana Revised
Statutes) read:

A school board also may authorize the proper school authorities . . . to allow each classroom teacher to ask if a student wishes to offer a prayer and, in the event no student does volunteer, to allow the teacher to offer a prayer. In no event shall any prayer last longer than five minutes. In no case may a student or a teacher be required to offer a prayer. Upon the objection of a student . . . or . . . of a parent . . . that student shall not be required to participate or be present in the classroom during the time a prayer is being offered.[3]

On December 3, 1980, a local school district, Jefferson Parish, established just such a program. Each school day was to begin with one minute of prayer and a minute of silent meditation. The school board made careful provisions to assure that student participation was voluntary. Only those students whose parents requested that their children participate were involved in this prayer time. The opening prayers were conducted under the supervision of a teacher who invited students to pray, or lacking volunteers, led the prayer.

Suit was brought against the school district (*Karen B.* v. *Treen*), and a U.S. district court upheld the school policies.

The judge, Adrian G. Duplantier, said that the requirement of parental permission helped "neutralize any appearance of government influence." He held that the statute did not aid or inhibit religion since the prayers could relate to anything—"from sports to the weather to religion." In fact, the judge said, the bill simply allowed the volunteer "to say something for one minute on any topic." He further declared:

. . . to hold that the Constitution . . . forbids prayer is to say that the Constitution espouses non-prayer or that it is hostile to prayer. . . .

If the Constitution prohibits those who believe in prayer from praying a prayer. . . then the Constitution impliedly teaches children that there is something wrong with prayer. . . .

I sum up by saying that in my view the Constitution guarantees freedom of religion, but should not be construed to guarantee freedom *from* religion. . . .

However, the Fifth Circuit Court of Appeals reversed his decision, and held that the Louisiana plan, like that in Massachusetts, violated the prohibitions of the First Amendment. The court held that there was no permissible secular purpose for the state to adopt the statute or for Jefferson Parish to implement it. There was instead an "obvious religious means." The court of appeals held that the elaborate methods to excuse students were irrelevant.

Appeals by Louisiana to the U.S. Supreme Court were rejected in January of 1982 when the Supreme Court declined to review the decisions.

So if you want school organized and arranged prayers, it will apparently take more than a statute. It is difficult to conceive that the courts will uphold any state statute that provides for school-structured prayers or prayer times. It will take an amendment, or a new set of Supreme Court justices with sharply different views of the Constitution!

CONGRESSIONAL ACTION

For this reason Congress has not been hesitant to get into the school prayer act. In fact, Senator Jesse Helms saw it as his "duty to insure that the freedoms protected by the First Amendment are not undermined by actions of other institutions."[4] No one in the Congress that day in December of 1980 was confused about the identity of those "other institutions." Helms obviously referred to the courts.

The "Helms Amendment," first suggested in 1979, is not a constitutional amendment but a proposal that attempts to restrict the power of federal courts to review cases dealing with "voluntary prayer." It is based on Article III of the Constitution, which allows Congress to limit the powers of the federal courts. The bill, titled the "Voluntary School Prayer Act of 1981," seeks to restore "the true spirit of the First Amendment" and the "fundamental right of voluntary prayer in the public schools."

Recently backed by the Prayer Project, a coalition of conservative political and religious groups, the bill reads:

Notwithstanding the provisions of sections

1253, 1254 and 1257 of this chapter the Supreme Court shall not have jurisdiction to review, by appeal, writ of certiorari, or otherwise, any case arising out of any State statute, ordinance, rule, regulations or any part thereof, or arising out of any act interpreting, applying, or enforcing a State statute, ordinance, rule or regulation which relates to voluntary prayers in public schools and public buildings.

For the purposes of this section, the term "voluntary prayer" shall not include any prayer composed by an official or any employee of a state or local governmental agency.[5]

Other sections apply the same restrictions to other federal courts.

The bill removes the power of the federal courts, including the Supreme Court, to review cases involving voluntary school prayer. While this approach may seem novel, the attempt to utilize this congressional power to overcome unpopular decisions of federal courts is neither new nor limited to school prayer. Between 1953 and 1963 alone, more than sixty bills were introduced that sought to remove federal jurisdiction over such subjects as legislative reapportionment, obscenity rulings, school busing, and abortion.

In 1979, the Helms Bill passed the Senate 50-41, but stalled in the House Judiciary Committee. The bill, however, re-emerged in 1981-82 and has created heated debate

Some, like Bob Dugan of the National Association of Evangelicals and Philip Crane, a representative from Illinois, have seen it as a legitimate exercise of congressional power. Crane, testifying at hearings with William Murray beside him, declared, "Congress needs a little more constitutional backbone. . . . [The Helms Bill] will supply a good stiff shot of calcium to Congress's rather gelatinous constitutional vertebrae."[6]

CRITICS WARN OF CONSEQUENCES

Not all like the idea. Laurence Tribe, professor at Harvard Law School, called the bill an "attempt to stack the deck."[7]

James Wood of the Baptist Joint Committee for Public Affairs (an independent lobbying organization with representation from most Baptist groups in America) saw an erosion of the whole Bill of Rights. The National Council of Churches called this effort to put issues concerning basic civil rights outside the Supreme Court's review "appalling," especially in the "sensitive and intimate area of religion."[8]

The United Methodist Church's General Conference in 1980 declared, "We are opposed to any attempt . . . to take away from the Supreme Court's jurisdiction decisions with respect to school prayer . . ."[9] The ACLU newsletter called the Helms Bill "a political attack on the federal bench unparalleled in history."[10]

IS THE HELMS BILL UNCONSTITUTIONAL?

While many were concerned about the wisdom of removing the review of national issues from the federal court system, others debated if the act itself was even constitutional. The Helms Bill is built on the provisions of Article III of the United States Constitution, which (in a clause referred to as the "exceptions clause") provides that:

> . . . the Supreme Court shall have appellate jurisdiction, both as to law and fact, *with such exceptions and under such regulations* as the Congress shall make [emphasis added].

Some scholars think that the whole process of removing a vital area of First Amendment issues from all federal courts is unconstitutional. The Supreme Court will declare it so if the Helms Bill passes, they say. Even the Reagan administration has argued against the Helms approach.

Other constitutional scholars such as Charles Rice of Notre Dame have argued enthusiastically for congressional power under Article III to determine what cases the federal court system may and may not hear. He believes that Congress is well within its powers to remove the federal court from hearing voluntary prayer cases. Charles Rice relies on the plain language of Article III and a 1868 case, *Ex parte McCardle*.

One noted legal scholar and advocate of judicial restraint, Raoul Berger, declares at the outset that he is "poles apart from

Senator Jesse Helms and . . . personally opposed to prayer in the schools.''[11] But he warns that one's views on the Helms Bill should not color one's interpretation of Congress's power. As unwise as Berger believes the move to be, Congress has the power to set such limits on the courts, even the Supreme Court. Attempts to limit the power of the Court or other government bodies is perfectly within the tradition of liberty, says Berger. The bill "merely seeks to restore self-rule to the states with respect to school prayer—an autonomy reserved to the states from the very beginning . . . exactly as the founders intended. . . . [We] should welcome the exercise of congressional power to restore the democratic system of government.''[12]

What would the impact of such a bill be if it were adopted? Obviously it is meant to encourage the states to adopt laws to permit the reintroduction of prayers in the schools.

However, two problems quickly emerge. First, all courts are subject to the law of the land, which has been determined by the Supreme Court. No court would be able to reverse the prayer decisions the Supreme Court has already made. The actual effect of barring federal courts and the Supreme Court from hearing school prayer cases would be to "freeze" the court decisions where they are now. The Supreme Court could not modify or reverse *Engel,* because it couldn't hear appeals from lower courts; therefore, the state courts would be bound to follow existing Supreme Court decisions barring prayers. Helms is probably expecting the state courts to find loopholes or "distinguishing" aspects in new prayer legislation, which would make the new legislation different from *Engel.*

The more serious question, however, is that the statute again avoids that difficult and slippery question of what *voluntary* means. Commentators have wondered: If the Court cannot hear cases involving "voluntary" prayers, could it not hear cases to decide whether or not certain practices were or were not "voluntary"? If that is so, would there really be any change? Could not the Court (consistent with its own decisions and those in Louisiana and Massachusetts) decide that policies legislators or school boards thought were "voluntary" were in fact involuntary, because of school involvement? Once these practices were involuntary, the Court could review them, and presumably strike them down as unconstitutional. Because of this, some feel that the word *voluntary* needs to be more clearly defined.

IS ALL PRAYER IN SCHOOL UNCONSTITUTIONAL?

In the cases we have discussed so far, the prayers all mentioned God. But what about "Godless" prayers? Are they constitutional?

When some parents in Illinois objected to a verse the kindergarten children said before their morning snack, the Elwood Public School of DeKalb deleted the word *God* from the poem.

The children then recited:

> We thank you for the flowers so sweet.
> We thank you for the food we eat.
> We thank you for the birds that sing.
> We thank you for everything.

Is that a prayer? Many of us would answer, "No!" But the court of appeals said, "Yes, it is prayer," and struck down the practice. The wall of separation between church and state must be kept "high and impregnable," the court said. Elwood Public School appealed to the Supreme Court, but they declined to review the decision.

If "Godless" prayers at the beginning of the day are impermissible, what about grace before lunch or snack times?

Next to "Now I lay me down to sleep . . ." the children's grace, "God is great; God is good. And we thank Him for our food," is probably one of the best known prayers in America. Parents in Whitestone, New York, objected when their children were not allowed to recite this simple grace because of a school board policy. A district court agreed with the parents. But the United States appeals court in *Stein* v. *Oshinsky* rejected the parents' claim. The parents will have to "content themselves with having their children say those prayers before nine or after three," the Court said.

However, a moment of silent meditation might be OK. In *Gaines* v. *Anderson*, the court upheld a Massachusetts statute that provided for a one-minute period of silence at the beginning of each school day. The court noted that no instruction to pray or meditate was associated with the statute, so it was neutral and permissible. However, where silent meditation statutes have included instructions to pray they have been ruled invalid.

What about students meeting on their own for prayer?

When the Supreme Court's decisions were first handed down, most people believed that the Court was not barring prayer, just state-sponsored prayer. In fact, as late as the 1980 hearings on the Helms Bill, many opponents of the bill declared that it was not necessary because the court had never banned "voluntary prayer."

Today it is not clear that voluntary prayer is alive and well. Of course, there is no bar to closing your eyes and thinking what you wish. But that would also be true even in an aggressively atheist state. Once you move beyond private thinking, courts and government officials, especially school administrators, have challenged students' attempts to meet together and pray on their own.

School officials in some instances have even told children they cannot bow their heads and say grace over meals, but these incidents have never developed into policies or lawsuits. Students in a Minnesota high school have also been advised not to gather at their lockers for prayer before school or in one instance told not to meet in their cars on school grounds. But again these seem to be isolated incidents.

Not so isolated, however, is the refusal of schools to allow religious students to meet in a classroom before school for prayer or Bible study. (Though a United States district court upheld a school policy in 1965 that permitted such activity, the trend now seems to be just the opposite.)

In the last couple of years a small group of students at Guilderland High School in New York State asked the principal if they could meet for prayer in a classroom before school started. The principal said, "No!" The local court said, "No!" And the court of appeals agreed. In fact, the court of appeals said such practices would be "too dangerous to permit." The Supreme Court refused to review this case (*Brandon* v. *Guilderland School District*), thus allowing this ban against the student activity to stand.

Students in Huntington Beach, California, did not fare any better. When they asked to meet in a high school classroom during lunch to study the Bible and pray, the principal and finally the California Court of Appeal ruled their activity would violate the constitutional requirement of separation of church and state. The court saw the opportunity to use the classroom "rent-free" as providing state aid to religion and putting state approval on a religious activity.

One school district did try to protect students' rights to meet for religious purposes on the same basis as other student organizations—the Lubbock, Texas, school district. Even after the Lubbock Civil Liberties Union sued the school district, the trial court upheld the policy of allowing Christian students to meet in school facilities. The court said the policy was neutral, because it permitted all types of student groups to gather.

But the court of appeals reversed this decision. Allowing religious meetings "at a time closely associated with the beginning or end of the school day implies recognition of religious activities," and carries with it "an implicit approval," the court of appeals ruled. Students in Lubbock, Texas, as in other parts of the country, may no longer meet together on school facilities as other student groups do. This case is now on appeal to the United States Supreme Court.

Engel struck down state-written prayers.

Schempp and *Murray* extended the prohibition to include the use of prescribed prayers and devotional exercises.

Now *Brandon* v. *Guilderland School District*, *Johnson* v. *Huntington Beach Union School District*, and *Lubbock Civil Liberties Union* v. *Lubbock Independent School District* have restricted the right of Christian students to meet and pray together before school or during lunch on school facilities. Student-initiated requests to pray also seem to have been outlawed.

Have our religious liberties been reduced to where one may: Hear no prayer. Speak no prayer. But still think a prayer?

Today students are free to engage in vigorous political dissent on school grounds (*Tinker* v. *Des Moines Independent Community School District*). They are free to write articles in student newspapers with only minimal school supervision. Students' civil rights are vigorously protected by the schools and by the American Civil Liberties Union. It seems ironic that schools are cracking down on a group of students who wish to quietly pray or read the Bible together. But this trend is well established. Courts are sustaining these restrictive policies.

One wonders: Where do we go from here?

PART TWO
A DEBATE

7

In God We Trust?

What does the Religion Clause of the First Amendment really mean? Some believe that the Religion Clause has been "turned upside down." One wonders how much the schools themselves have contributed to a one-sided view of the First Amendment. Try to remember your junior high school civics class. What were you taught about the First Amendment? How often did you hear the familiar words *separation of church and state* or *a wall of separation between church and state*?

And what interpretation was given to this slogan? Did the church seem to be kept from influencing or participating in activities and policies of the state? Did a teacher mention that the words *wall* and *separation* do not occur in the First Amendment?

Thomas Jefferson coined the unforgettable phrase "wall of separation" in a letter he wrote to the Danbury Baptists, who had attacked him during a presidential campaign, calling him an infidel and an atheist.

> Believing that religion is a matter which lies solely between man and his God, and that he owes account to none other for his faith or his worship . . . I contemplate with sovereign reverence that act of the whole American people which declared that their legislature should "make no law respecting an establishment of religion or prohibiting the free exercise thereof," thus building a wall of separation between church and state.

76

Jefferson might have meant to silence the Danbury Baptists. But one would doubt that he meant to keep Jews and Christians from expressing their views for the rest of American history. Such a view of a "wall" did not appear in the First Amendment; in fact, Jefferson was in Europe when the amendment was written. Many historians feel that the framers' view of a wall of separation, if they did see a wall, was closer to that envisioned by Rhode Island's founder, Roger Williams—a wall to protect the church from government:

> . . . when they have opened a gap in the hedge
> or wall of separation between the garden of the
> church and the wilderness of the world, God
> hath ever broke down the wall itself . . . and
> made His garden a wilderness, as at this day.
> . . . [I]f He will e'er please to restore His
> garden and paradise again, it must of necessity
> be walled in peculiarly unto Himself from the
> world.

Williams saw the need to protect the church from government. As Christians we need to rethink our own interpretation of the First Amendment and realize that it was meant to protect our religious freedom from any invasion by the secular state. All too often we placidly accept an infringement of our religious liberty when someone utters the "sacred" words *separation of church and state*. The reaction is ingrained. After all, it began years ago when we studied civics and United States history.

A LOOK AT HISTORY

Further evidence of the framer's intention in the Religion Clause can be seen by looking at the environment in which they lived. The early colonies were suffused with religion. Nine of the states at the time of the Constitution had established churches. The Continental Congress authorized regular chaplains, and in 1788 Congress provided salaries for them.[1] And the Northwest Ordinance of 1787 (Article 3) provided for schools and the means of education, noting that "religion, morality and knowledge [are] necessary to good government and the happiness of mankind."[2]

The Treaty of Peace with Great Britain in 1783 began "In

the name of the Most Holy and Undivided Trinity . . ." And an early Congress authorized the importation of 20,000 Bibles into the new country. When the vote was seven states to six, however, the majority modified the resolution to encourage the individual states to import Bibles.

Washington's "Farewell Address" linked the religious faith of the nation to its republican institutions and warned against believing that morality can be maintained without religion. Refined education alone will be insufficient, Washington said, for both reason and experience "forbid us to expect that national morality can prevail in exclusion of religious principle."[3] Alexis de Tocqueville, the noted French observer of American life, concurred, noting that he was sure Americans held religion as "indispensable to the maintenance of republican institutions." Even Thomas Jefferson observed that Virginia supported various kinds of religion "to preserve peace and order [and] morals."[4]

In 1815 Justice Joseph Story of the United States Supreme Court spoke again of the positive relationship between religion and government, noting:

> Every American colony, from its foundation to
> the revolution . . . did openly, by the whole
> course of its law and institutions, support and
> sustain in some form the Christian religion.
> . . . Probably at the time of the Constitution
> and of the [first] amendment . . . the general if
> not the universal sentiment in America was,
> that Christianity ought to receive encourage-
> ment from the State. . . . And indeed all the
> state constitutions except West Virginia's con-
> tain tributes to God.[5]

De Tocqueville wasn't the only foreign observer who saw the American experiment as linked to a religious commitment. Karl Marx, writing in 1844, referred to America as "peculiarly the land of religiosity."[6]

A host of government acts have borne witness to this religious heritage. On April 22, 1864, Congress adopted the Coinage Act, which put In God We Trust on all United States coins.[7] In 1948, Congress passed a statute requiring every federal justice or judge to take an oath that concluded with the words *so help me God*. In 1954 Congress amended the Pledge of Allegiance, adding the words *under God*. The committee recommending the amendment noted that since the flag is symbolic of our nation and the morality of its people, it is "most appropriate that the concept of God be included." This was not establishing religion, the committee said, since we are simply declaring our belief in the sovereignty of God and not establishing any institution of religion. The phrase "under God recognizes only the guidance of God in our national affairs."

In 1952 Congress called on the president to proclaim annually a National Day of Prayer. And every president since Washington, except for Jefferson and Jackson, have issued Presidential Thanksgiving Proclamations. Wilson began his by saying, "America was born a Christian nation. America was born to exemplify that devotion to the elements of righteousness which are derived from the Holy Scriptures."[8]

On July 11, 1955, President Dwight D. Eisenhower signed Public Law 140, requiring *In God We Trust* on all currency, and a year later Public Law 851 declared In God We Trust as our national motto. That motto is engraved over the south door of the United States Senate. At one point a bill was introduced to inscribe the words above the bench of the Supreme Court, but Chief Justice Earl Warren objected.

Kennedy's 1962 proclamation that set aside a Day of Prayer bears, Charles Rice noted, striking similarities to the New York Regents' Prayer, which was banned that very year. Note the parallels:

> Regents' Prayer:
> Almighty God, we acknowledge our dependence on Thee, and we beg Thy blessing on us, our parents, our teachers and our country.

> Kennedy's Proclamation:
> Whereas faith in Almighty God was a dominant power in the Lives of our Founding Fathers; and
> Whereas they expressed this faith in prayer . . . and
> Whereas in full recognition of our dependence

upon Almighty God . . .
Now therefore . . . may we especially ask God's
blessing upon—
Our homes . . .
Our citizens . . .
Our nation . . .
And our world. . . .

All of this seems to reinforce Justice William O. Douglas's statement in *Zorach* v. *Clauson* (which upheld off-campus religious education for students who were released from school). "We are a religious people whose institutions presuppose the existence of a Supreme Being." And, as United States Congressman James H. Quillen (R-Tenn.) put it, "We are a religious people who would like to stay that way."[9]

In *Zorach*, Justice Douglas argued that schools ought to accommodate the religious beliefs of students, because this is in keeping with the very best of our traditions, which have always recognized the existence of God and sought his counsel in the affairs of our nation.

Why, then, should schools not acknowledge this tradition? To even begin to answer this question, we need to look to other elements of our tradition and ask a few questions of our own. Was America really as thoroughly Christian as some suggest? Is she still? Or has the religious consensus been largely diluted into a pluralistic sentiment?

FROM PURITANS TO MORAL MAJORITY

It is critical to recognize that the religious character of America has increasingly broadened from the specific doctrinal interests in colonial days to Protestantism, then to Christianity, and then to a more general Judeo-Christian focus. Today groups like the Moral Majority seek an even broader consensus, built around common moral commitments without any necessary doctrinal commonality. The public recognition of religion has become gradually less specific as the nation has become more pluralistic.

A number of factors moved the early governments away from sectarianism. In order to grow commercially, the new government, and especially New England, had to increase their contact with those who were not the "elect." Further, new immigrants who did not come to America with the specific religious mission of the New England colonials gradually outnumbered groups like the orthodox Puritans. Other religious groups like the Catholics diversified the doctrinal beliefs of the new country.

Once a unified government was formed to defend America during the Revolutionary War, the government became even less sectarian in its religion. General Washington, for example, urged his army not to participate in New England's traditional "Pope's Day," a celebration in which the pope was burned in effigy.[10]

THE FAITH OF OUR FOUNDING FATHERS?

Contrary to what many are led to believe by the religious rhetoric of the colonial period, religious patterns had significantly changed by revolutionary days. Not only were a good many of the revolutionary leaders more deist than Christian, but the actual number of church members was rather small. Perhaps as few as 5 percent of the populace were church members in 1776. The percentage tripled by 1850, and has tripled again in modern times.[11]

James Dunn, director of the Baptist Joint Committee for Public Affairs, says the founding fathers may have been persons of faith, but they certainly would not be "acceptable in most evangelical churches today." In fact they were, Dunn insists, more like secular humanists with their talk of "liberty, fraternity and equality" and the "triumph of the human spirit." Many, like Thomas Jefferson and James Madison, were products of the Enlightenment rather than of biblical principles.

Ethan Allen, the hero in the capture of Fort Ticonderoga, declared that "prayer is no part of a rational religion." And Thomas Paine said that churches were "inventions set up to terrify and enslave." John Adams declared the world would be best if there were no religion in it. Jefferson said Christianity and other "superstitions of the world" were "founded on fables and mythologies," and so he created his own "wee little book"—a Bible revised by the heavy use of scissors and paste to eliminate the doctrines and passages (such as miracles) he found objectionable.

I have noted the heavy religious language of the Treaty of Peace with Britain, but a few years later, a treaty with Tripoli offered a different appraisal in its preamble. "As the government of the United States is not, in any sense, founded on the Christian religion . . ."[12]

Today one can even find a secularized version of the motto In God We Trust on a counter sign in a discount food chain. The black placard by the cash register declares:

In God we trust
Everyone else pays in cash.

Surely the secularization of our country is complete.

MADALYN WASN'T FIRST

Movements to minimize government support of religion did not begin with Madalyn Murray O'Hair. Even though the majority of Americans have held to a theistic core, some dissent was expressed. In 1867, for example, the Free Religious Association was founded, which published a series of demands in January of 1874. The association called for an end to tax exemptions for churches, tax support of chaplains, the use of the Bible in public schools, the designation of religious holidays, judicial oaths, Sunday observances, and laws enforcing Christian morality.[13]

THE MYTH OF RELIGIOUS TOLERANCE

Although the early colonists came to America to seek religious freedom, they were not particularly tolerant of others. Those who fled to Cape Cod for freedom and signed the Mayflower Compact also exiled Roger Williams for his views on the rights of conscience and his opposition to a colonial statute that penalized Quakers.

Virginia's first charter, in 1606, noted that the "propagation of Christian religion" was one of its purposes. But for all its religious beliefs, Virginia proscribed Quakers as "pestilent heretics" and provided the death penalty for practicing the Catholic faith.[14] Article 95 of the Fundamental Constitution of Carolina in 1669 provided, "No man shall be permitted to be a freeman of Carolina . . . that doth not acknowledge a God, and that God is publicly and solemnly to be worshipped."

THEREFORE?

It seems difficult to build a case for government sponsored

prayer solely on an appeal to our religious history. That history is too mixed and confused, containing not only moments of glory, but also some sadder episodes—stories of intolerance and intimidation. Neither is our history distinctively Christian in an evangelical sense. The commitment to a moral order was there, and in the main a strong acknowledgment of theism. But evangelical, born-again Christianity had far less appeal than today. The common religion was more akin to contemporary liberalism.

One wonders if the history of our nation's experience with religion argues for avoiding government involvement rather than supporting it. It is striking that in the colonial days, when government subsidized churches, a relatively small percentage of Americans were involved in church life. Today, with a more formal separation, the vigor of evangelical Christianity is apparent. Has a decline in form perhaps led to a recovery of substance?

8

Shouldn't the Majority Rule?

Suppose a pollster asks you to give your opinion on the school prayer issue. Two of the initial statements might be:

> If participation in school prayer is voluntary, it does not violate a student's rights.
>
> _____ Yes _____ No

> If the majority of Americans want school prayer, it's OK.
>
> _____ Yes _____ No

You probably answered yes in both situations. After all, if school prayer is voluntary and the majority says it's OK, what's all the fuss about, anyway? But before you or I answer such questions, we need to take a closer look at the issues and the questions we are being asked.

Let's begin with the word *voluntary*. We have already discussed the dictionary meaning of the word. Now let's see what "voluntary" prayer might mean in the classroom.

In hearings on the Helms Bill, Robert M. McClory (R-Ill.) observed:

> One of the key questions this subcommittee is going to have to probe is what is, in fact, meant by "voluntary"? The questions that this subcommittee will have to try and answer are: Who

should conduct the prayer exercise? A student? A teacher? A minister? What should be the age of the participants? Should such a prayer be conducted in the classroom? Should it be conducted during the regular class hours or otherwise? Should the "volunteers" be told they can assemble or should they be told they can leave? Should someone be there to observe whether school authorities or the teachers express approval or disapproval of those participating in the prayer? Should the prayer exercises be offered as a part of the school routine or should [they] be left to student initiative during free time such as study period or recess?[1]

Some have suggested that the Helms approach and the constitutional amendment are unnecessary because voluntary prayer has never been outlawed by the courts. Yet, as we have seen, the courts have struck down statutes in Massachusetts and Louisiana that purported to be voluntary prayer schemes. And more disturbingly, the truly voluntary prayers of students in Huntington Beach and Guilderland High School were stopped. Even in *Engel* and *Schempp*, no one was compelled to participate in the prayers. Isn't that voluntary?

The issue of voluntariness has plagued the discussion of cases and proposed practices ever since the Supreme Court struck down the Regents' Prayer in 1962. From the courts' perspective, certain practices that some have defined as voluntary are really not—at least that's the way the courts seemed to apply the First Amendment.

"And You May Leave the Room . . ."

The courts have argued that voluntariness is not achieved by the teacher merely announcing, "If you do not wish to participate in devotions, you may leave the room." The courts have taken special note of the character of the public school, the authority of its structures, and the weight of the teacher's choices and suggestions. School activity carries with it a pressure to participate, especially when small children are involved. Pressure is not viewed in a physical or technical sense, but in a social and psychological context.

Richard Cohen, writing in the *Washington Post*, said:

> There is simply nothing voluntary about it.
> When you're eight years old and everyone
> around you bows their head, you bow your
> head. When everyone is mumbling words, you
> mumble words. . . . And you do this not
> because you want to, but because you do not
> want to make a spectacle of yourself.[2]

The dilemma between a child's faithfulness to parental
religious teachings and peer and teacher pressure exposes a child
to the "cruelest turmoil," according to Rabbi Polish of the
Synagogue Council of America. When the state organizes the activity, it simply "can never be truly voluntary," insisted Samuel
Rabinove of the American Jewish Committee during congressional testimony.

Long before *Engel*, state courts had sensed this. In 1890 the
Wisconsin Supreme Court (in *ex rel. Weiss* v. *District Board*)
prohibited school prayers that were said to be voluntary. And in
1910, the Illinois Supreme Court declared, "exclusion of a pupil
from this part of the school exercises . . . separates him from his
fellows, puts him in a class by himself, deprives him of his
equality . . . [and] subjects him to a religious stigma" (*People ex
rel Ring* v. *Board of Education*). The Louisiana Supreme Court
agreed later, declaring, "excusing school children . . . would
work a discrimination. [It] puts him in a class by himself . . .
and all because of his religious beliefs" (*Herold* v. *Parish Board
of School Directors*).

Even in *Karen B.* v. *Treen* where the Jefferson, Louisiana,
school system created a program of voluntary prayer at the
beginning of the school day for students who had parental approval, the voluntariness did not save the plan because of the
significant level of the school's involvement. A series of factors
seem to have been persuasive: the potential for embarrassment
to students who choose not to participate, the requirement that
those with contrary religious views publicly identify themselves
and be isolated, and the potential for division and conflict for
religious reasons, which has no part in the public schools. The
court also saw a need to respect the diversities of religious traditions and practices.

Some courts, however, have realized that nowadays "the shoe is often on the other foot"; it may be more embarrassing for a child to be labeled "religious" than "irreligious." In *People ex. rel Vollmer* v. *Stanley*, the Colorado Supreme Court said, "We have known many boys to be ridiculed for complying with religious regulations but never one for neglecting or absenting himself from them."

One might note that the courts' statements that students will experience peer pressure if they don't participate in school prayer are often based on assumptions and not testimony. Or even more disturbingly, on hypothetical possibilities. For example, in *Brandon*, where the court rejected the rights of students to meet for prayer, the court expressed concern about student intimidation—without a shred of evidence to that effect. Those who visit schools today and Christian children in secular schools would testify that young people are more likely to risk ridicule if they are a part of prayer or devotions than if they refuse to participate.

Of course, the schools should not seek to provide a conflict-free environment, insulating children from exposure to inevitable differences, even possible embarrassment or ridicule for their views. Schools should not see ideological neutrality or conformity as a high goal of education, Justice Robert Jackson noted in *McCollum*. "It may be doubted whether the Constitution . . . protects one from the embarrassment that always attends non-conformity, whether in religion, politics, behaviour or dress," he said. But he added that it is different when the conformity is created by the direct acts of the state in promoting certain religious practices.

What is voluntary? Certainly the more the state is involved in structuring and managing the prayer times, the less likely true choices are being made by students. Perhaps, therefore, the courts have been correct in ruling that prayer, when the school writes or prescribes it or includes the devotions as part of the school day, is not voluntary.

And in cases such as *Engel* and *Schempp*, the courts have declared voluntariness irrelevant. The Constitution, they say, prohibits government-sponsored religion, even if everyone wants it.

But when the initiative comes from the students, the prayers are written or prayed extemporaneously by the students, and the events are not part of the school's structured academic day (such as before school or at lunchtime or on other student discretionary time), the allegations that use of school facilities destroys voluntary participation seems forced. One could just as well argue that a student is unable to choose not to eat lunch, just because the food in the school cafeteria is provided by school employees.

THE MAJORITY RULES?

Seventy-nine percent of Americans favor President Reagan's prayer proposal, according to a Gallup Poll taken on June 10, 1982. Only 16 percent opposed a prayer amendment. And 82 percent of those polled had heard of the president's prayer proposal, which is not bad exposure for one of many statements issued from the Rose Garden.

"If the majority rules, and the majority wants prayer in the schools, then it's OK," some may reason. But there may be more to consider here than just the majority opinion.

On July 12, 1962, one month after the Supreme Court's decision on prayer, the Baptist Press wrote an editorial that ought to give us all pause:

> Nobody will admit it, but resentment against Jews, freethinkers, Unitarians and atheists goes a long way to explain the negative reaction of many people against the Supreme Court. While it is true, and perhaps unfortunate, that many of the cases involving religious liberty have been initiated by minority and unpopular groups, it is not true that these groups are imposing their views on the American people.
>
> Basic principles of American life should be decided on principle. Reactions to decisions should be made on the basis of right and wrong rather than prejudice.[3]

Perhaps the Baptist Press was right in noting an undercurrent of prejudice. It may function not only against the Supreme Court decisions but also against those who may resist the reinstitution of school prayers.

Let's look at the potential for school prayer to create

dissension between religious communities and most tragically between Christians and Jews. A Jesuit editorial in *America* magazine after the Supreme Court's prayer decision was entitled "To Our Jewish Friends." Its antagonistic tone was probably inspired by the fact that two of the five families involved in the prayer cases were Jewish, and that the New York Board of Rabbis had enthusiastically endorsed the Court's decision. The editorial warned that "certain spokesmen and leaders in the Jewish community . . . are now taking steps to consolidate the 'gains' which were made through the decision." The editorial complained of the "all-out campaign to secularize the public schools" on the part of a few Jewish organizations and concluded:

> The time has come for these fellow citizens of ours to decide among themselves precisely what they conceive to be the final objective of the Jewish community in the United States. . . . When court victories produce only a harvest of fear and distrust, will it all have been worthwhile?[4]

The Jewish groups implicated in the editorial responded quickly. Rabbi Elmer Berger of the American Council for Judaism declared, "*America* performs a disservice in raising the spectre of anti-Semitism," and the Central Conference of American Rabbis called the editorial "threatening and patronizing."

A more recent example of hidden feelings coming to light was the exchange in a 1981 Senate debate over school prayer. Senator Hollings (D-S.C.), arguing for school prayer, referred to his opponent in the debate, Senator Howard Metzenbaum, as "the Senator from B'nai B'rith." Hollings later apologized.

It is no secret that with few exceptions the Jewish community has been the most disturbed by school prayer formalities and has taken a major role in court cases and congressional testimony against such efforts. Rabbi Arthur Gibert notes that this resistance emerges from a "historic fear that the Jewish community feels with regard to Christian imposition." Gibert admits that though the Jewish community will use the language of the law to explain its objections, the real factors are a "combination of fear, historic memory and the secularization of the Jewish community."[5]

When the Supreme Court decisions first came down, criticism of the Court's "nit-picking" about discrimination against minorities was widespread. Many, like *America* magazine, argued that our whole cultural and religious tradition was being shifted because of the complaints of a few people who just ought to be less cantankerous. Majorities have rights, too, people felt. William Ball, a well-known constitutional attorney, in a debate in the sixties with separationist Leo Pfeffer, said, "the Supreme Court has apparently written all interested pressure groups a stack of blank checks." He warned that when they were cashed, "as little may be left of inter-religious goodwill in the USA as Sherman left in Georgia."

Constitutional lawyer Charles Rice sided with Ball, and argued that the Court has "paid an eccentric deference to the inflated scruples of a small minority, preferring them over the views of the vast majority."[6]

SYMPATHY FOR MINORITY RIGHTS

Certainly, issues of the rights of majorities and minorities are complex questions, not just for constitutional adjudication, but in a larger political and philosophic sense. On the one hand, a nation must proclaim its essential character and values in the face of opposition. The body politic does create an ethos, a common system of belief, which the community will seek to perpetuate.

On the other hand, our government's ethos includes, at least as the Supreme Court has viewed it, a commitment not to discriminate on the basis of religion or interfere with its free exercise. So central is the issue of minority rights and feelings that Richard Cohen, writing in the *Washington Post* in 1981, said school prayer is about the "sensitivities of minorities."

Indeed, Christians need to learn to be more sensitive to minority interests, especially when those interests emerge out of deeply held religious sensibilities. Of all people, Christians ought to understand the need to be totally obedient to the dictates of one's conscience and one's religious commitments. There is enough history of persecution of both Christians and Jews in the world to create a common bond, a commitment to resist all government attempts to pressure people toward religious affirmations or impose religious exercises on people.

Christians simply must become aware of the emotional and practical consequences of being a minority people. That lesson is critical, not only so that minorities may be treated with respect, but so that our own "strangeness" and "alienism" (which are clear biblical themes) may not be lost.

The test of religious liberty, after all, is not whether the majority is treated with respect and granted freedom, but whether those with minimal political or cultural influence are treated justly. While majorities have rights, imposing their religious views on the minority is not one of them, nor is using their political power to enlist the assistance of the government in such an endeavor. This was Justice Tom Clark's point in *Schempp:*

> Finally, we do not accept that the concept of neutrality . . . collides with the majority's right of free exercise of religion. While the Free Exercise Clause clearly prohibits the use of state action to deny the rights of free exercise to anyone, it has never meant that the majority could use the machinery of the state to practice its beliefs.

The Court then quoted from the famous flag-salute case, *West Virginia Board of Education* v. *Barnette*, in which the Court held that West Virginia could not compel young Barnette to salute the flag against his religious belief. In that case, the majority had argued its rights. But some issues were beyond mere momentary majorities, the Court declared:

> The very purpose of the Bill of Rights was to withdraw certain subjects from the vicissitudes of political controversy, to place them beyond the reach of majorities and officials and establish them as legal principles. . . . One's right to . . . freedom of worship . . . and other fundamental rights may not be submitted to vote; they depend on the outcome of no election.

Surely that seems sound. We have committed ourselves as a

people to the principle of free exercise; certain rights are not infringed—not even by the power of democratic vote. It has been suggested that laws are made by men in their best moments to protect themselves from themselves in their worst moments. Perhaps that is what a constitution is: protecting ourselves in our better moments from letting our less charitable instincts govern.

It would be especially tragic for Christians, who are a pilgrim people, fighting in most parts of the globe for equality and freedom, to use government power to force our views on the minority peoples in this land. It's bad law. It's bad gospel.

9

Has God Really
Been Expelled from School?

The need for "wholesome neutrality" on the part of the state toward religion was the Supreme Court's chief argument against school prayer in *Abington* v. *Schempp*. The Court declared that both the prohibition against the establishment of religion (in the Establishment Clause) and the commitment not to interfere with the religious practices of citizens (under the Free Exercise Clause) required policies that neither supported nor disparaged any religious faith.

As attractive as neutrality sounds, many have argued that it is a myth. "[E] stablished neutrality is impossible. . . . [It is the] first step to established hostility," testified Carl McIntyre, a Presbyterian minister, to a congressional committee in the early days of the school prayer disputes. There will always be some informing philosophy, some religion underlying education. It cannot be neutral, so which world view shall it be?

Twenty years before *Schempp*, Dr. George Johnson, of the Commission on American Citizenship, wrote an introduction to a curriculum series in which he declared:

> It is impossible to be neutral in the wake of
> religion . . . the very conviction that religion
> can be left out of the curriculum assumes tacitly
> that the things of God are not as essential to
> human well being as the things of the world. Bit
> by bit, this tacit assumption has been an explicit

93

doctrine with the consequent acceptance of
secularism as the basis of American educational
policy.[1]

A *Texas Tech Law Review* article speaks of the Court's
neutrality as a "hopeful illusion," which is unattainable since all
law assumes a moral principle. Charles Rice, professor of law at
Notre Dame, referred to the Court's search for neutrality as a
"vain thing," which only substituted a "new agnostic premise
entailing a perpetual suspension of judgment on the part of
government as to the existence of God" for the traditional
theistic premise.[2]

The possibility of neutrality running amok was acknowledged by the concurring opinion of Justice Arthur Goldberg in
Schempp. Goldberg warned that an "untutored devotion to the
concept of neutrality [might] lead to . . . a brooding and per-
vasive devotion to the secular and a passive, or even active,
hostility to the religious."

SECULAR HUMANISM

A noted constitutional scholar of the church/state question,
Paul Kauper, noted that in seeking neutrality a "tightrope"
must be walked to avoid a secularist philosophy, which is a
"religion by default."[3]

It's a tightrope that has not been navigated, many allege.

The popular description of the religion of secularism that
our schools have implicitly adopted is *secular humanism*. The
phrase has been used so broadly and uncritically that it may no
longer be useful. But I will try to define it.

In its essence, secular humanism developed out of the
classical humanism of the Greeks and Romans. It builds upon
the idea that man is the measure of all things. It emphasizes
man's rationality and ridicules the supernatural and religion as
impediments to human progress. Secular humanism's hope for
the future rests not on any god, but on man himself as he solves
his own problems. Man has taken the place of God, for man
looks to no values or truths as absolute but his own.

Many believe that the secular state (a legitimately
nonreligious body) has become this sort of humanistic state, em-
bracing the presuppositions of agnosticism, if not atheism.

Many draw attention to the "doctrinal statement" of this

virulent humanism—the Humanist Manifesto I and II—and have found parallels between the philosophic presuppositions of those documents and the principles employed in modern education. This religion of secular humanism, though professing to be nonreligious, liberal, and open-minded, is intolerant of opposing views. Harvey Cox, of the Harvard Divinity School, noted this intolerance and declared, "[the view is] opposed to other religions; it actively rejects, excludes, and attempts to eliminate traditional theism from meaningful participation in the American culture."[4]

THE FAMOUS FOOTNOTE

Perhaps the most famous reference to the religious nature of secular humanism is a footnote that was appended to the Supreme Court case, *Torcaso* v. *Watkins*, a decision that preceded the prayer cases by one year. A Maryland ordinance that required a notary public to declare a belief in the existence of God as part of an oath of office was held unconstitutional. The decision itself was not surprising, but a footnote in the majority opinion will keep the case in the public eye for years.

Justice Hugo Black noted that the state can neither pass laws favoring particular religions nor favor religion as opposed to irreligion. Nor can the state favor religions that believe in the existence of God over those religions founded on different beliefs. At that point a footnote appeared:

> Among the religions in this country which do not teach what would generally be considered a belief in the existence of God are Buddhism, Taoism, Ethical Culture, Secular Humanism, and others.

Did the Court hold that secular humanism is a religion? Well, at least, it could be—if one can find the slippery thing. It certainly did not say every idea held by secularists or humanists was a religious view.

Many, like Francis Schaeffer, claim that secular humanism is a religion, and that the schools—or some curricular components—express the religious views of this humanism. Such views are, therefore, impermissible because they violate the prohibition against the establishment of a religion.

The Court certainly has held that where persons have a belief system that binds their conduct and conscience in the same way traditional religious belief does, their beliefs are entitled to the privileges of religious belief (*Seeger* v. *U.S.*). The consequences of such a view are enormous. As Paul Kauper asks, "[I]f the schools consciously engage in a program of indoctrination in ethical values, resting on humanistic considerations, are they thereby contributing to the promotion and establishment of religion in the public schools?"[5]

Of course, if this argument is pushed to an extreme, all moral teaching would be eliminated from public education. And if a loose similarity in content between the views of avowed secular humanists and school teaching is sufficient to bar its use, moral teaching in keeping with Christian thought would also be illegal.

Something more than a mere convergence of ideas will have to be shown to prove that public schools are teaching a religion. Can it? Many say yes, and cite some values clarification programs and/or sex education curricula as evidence of a conscious philosophic commitment so thorough and comprehensive that it is a world view, which is often deliberately contrary to Christian thought. Lawsuits have been filed in a number of cases seeking to obtain court adjudication that secular humanism has been established in the school systems, but so far those cases have been unsuccessful.

This author believes that there is an increasingly hostile atmosphere in public education that sometimes does amount to a secular humanist bias, but I caution Christians to be careful of several fallacies as they strive to prove this point. First, there is a tendency to use the label "secular humanism" merely to attack unpopular ideas, literature, and techniques in a careless way. Not all programs we dislike are part of a world view that is hostile to religion. Secondly, the vast majority of teachers do not hold a consistent world view of secular humanism (or perhaps any other world view). Even those who may have been significantly influenced by its thought are not necessarily captured by it. Thirdly, judicial remedies in this area are almost certain to be ineffective. It will be difficult to link specific curricular programs to a comprehensive world view that has the clear attributes of a religious philosophy.

Furthermore, courts are not likely to hold that the prevailing educational system is impermissible. Can you imagine the headlines? "Supreme Court Rules American School Systems Unconstitutional." The ensuing chaos would make good fiction, but it would be far from productive for American education.

Could school prayer be an effective antidote to humanistic education? I doubt it. While an official prayer time might provide one suggestion that man is *not* the measure of all things, it is unlikely that a brief, often perfunctory and ritualistic, ceremony can fight this massive philosophic undertow. The issue is not really whether or not a few minutes ought to be given to God, but rather how to combat the basic philosophy of a godless universe. If the heart is diseased, a little bandage is not likely to do much good.

WHAT ABOUT MORALITY?

If God has been expelled from American schools, is there still some morality in public education? Many of us still agree with Alexis de Tocqueville, who observed American life in its political infancy and said: "America is great because she is good, and if America ever ceases to be good, America will cease to be great."

Many still believe that "righteousness exalteth a nation," and that morality and greatness are inseparably linked. Morality is not in the sphere of private life alone, but it is a function of public life as well. Certainly the last few decades have seen moral issues raised to prominence in public life: desegregation, protection of the environment, criminal justice, concern for the poor, human rights. These are causes that elicit support not because they are "cost effective" or popular, but because their advocates believe them to be morally obligatory.

If morality is a part of our public life and a part of personal integrity, then it surely must be included in education and the functions of public education. Furthermore, if education includes morality, it must include religion to some degree, for religion provides not only the "rules" of morality, but the basis on which to assert the moral category.

Frank Sheed in *Society and Sanity* noted how "grotesque" any educational effort would be that had no notion of what man is or what life is for. He charged public education in the West with precisely that failing. Yet as odd as it is, it does not strike people as odd. "[T]he depth of their unawareness is the measure of our decay of thinking about fundamentals," Sheed noted.[6]

Alfred North Whitehead, the famed philosopher, put it most directly: "The essence of education is that it be religious." Former Villanova Dean Gianella took the next step: "Since education touches directly on religious concerns, such as the meaning of existence and the sources and nature of human values, once the state assumes a dominant role in this area it must take religion into account immediately."[7]

RELIGION AND EDUCATION IN AMERICA

"In Adam's fall / We sinned all." A line from a hymn? A catechism? Couldn't come from a school textbook? Or could it? The *New England Primer* used couplets such as this to teach language and alphabets to children. It wasn't unusual, for education in colonial America was intimately bound up with religion. The schools were not public in the contemporary sense. Even at the time of independence, the typical school was most often denominational, operated by such groups as Puritans, Anglicans, Quakers, or Moravians. These schools received considerable financial support from the public treasury. Even secular subjects were taught with a vigorous religious flavor. The primer included the Lord's Prayer, the Apostle's Creed, and a version of the catechism.

In 1787 Congress even set aside two sections of land in each township specifically for the development of a university. At that time, universities, such as Yale, Harvard, Princeton, Rutgers, and Dartmouth, were almost totally dedicated to preparing ministers.

As the nation developed, the schools tended to be less sectarian, though maintaining much of their religious flavor. State constitutional provisions for education often linked it to religion. The North Carolina constitutional provision for schools, for example, declared that schools were needed "whereby the rising generation may be brought up and instructed in the principles of the Christian religion."[8]

Gradually the public school began to experience the same kind of secularization that the nation itself went through. A key figure in the development of schools was Horace Mann in Massachusetts. Under his leadership, the public school movement expanded. He was an advocate of the nonsectarian character of public schools and of public financial support for nonsectarian rather than sectarian education. But though he was a relative "secularist," he was convinced that the Bible served an important public purpose in education and the schools.

In his valedictory address to the people of Massachusetts after he had served as commissioner of education for twelve years, Mann noted that schools were barred from inculcating particular doctrines of any one religious denomination. "But our system earnestly inculcates all Christian morals; it founds its morals on the basis of religion; it welcomes the religion of the Bible; and, in receiving the Bible, it allows it to do what it is allowed to do in no other system, to speak for itself."[9]

In a letter in 1844 Horace Mann declared his wish for the Bible to continue to be used in the schools. It "makes known to us the rule of life and the means of salvation."

John Dewey, who along with Mann is probably the most familiar name associated with education, was far less sympathetic to religion than Mann was. Dewey is perhaps the philosophic founder of current education. He was critical of religion and theistic belief, insisting that the democratic ideal required the "surrender" of a belief in God. In fact he was one of the drafters and signers of the first Humanist Manifesto, issued in 1933.

But despite the gradually shrinking religious content in education, different faiths still fought over theological matters. Catholics frequently resisted religious exercises in public schools. When Massachusetts became the first state to actually enact a law requiring public school Bible reading in 1855, Catholics opposed the statute. (Interestingly, it wasn't until 1910 that any other state required the practice of devotional exercises, Alabama following Massachusetts in 1910, and ten more states by 1913.)[10]

In Massachusetts the statute didn't stop religious conflict. In 1866 the Supreme Court of Massachusetts approved the expelling of a girl who refused to bow her head during the devotional exercises. Similar results occurred in Iowa in 1884 and Kansas in 1904. Even as late as 1950, Catholics objected to the Protestant character of the observances. But a New Jersey court held that ". . . the Old Testament and the Lord's Prayer, pronounced without comment, are not sectarian . . ."[11]

In 1946 Father Connell, assistant professor at Catholic University, advised Catholic teachers to "avoid the Protestant

Bible if possible" and bring their own Bible to class. He also counseled against reciting the phrase "For thine is the Kingdom . . ." in the Lord's Prayer, since it has a "Protestant connotation" and repeating it would "constitute an implicit approval of heresy."[12]

Perhaps the most tragic story of struggle over religion in the public schools occurred in 1843 and 1844. In 1843 Bishop Francis Kenrick of Philadelphia petitioned the school board, asking that Roman Catholic children be allowed to use the Roman Catholic version of the Bible. Apparently the school board approved. The Native American political faction, an anti-immigrant group, resented the request and the board's acquiescence, and accused the Catholics of trying to ban the King James Bible from the schools. Several months of controversy exploded into rioting. One Catholic church was attacked and two others burned, and then the riots extended into the Italian section, where a number of homes were destroyed and a number of persons killed.

The reports of the Philadelphia rioting caused Bishop Hughes of New York to close his churches as he sought laws against the required reading of the "Protestant Bible."[13] The struggle in New York resulted in an estimate by Governor Seward that perhaps one-fourth to one-fifth of the children of New York were without education for several years, because Catholic parents kept their children at home.[14]

To all these challenges the American and Foreign Christian Union replied that the Bible would not be expelled from the classrooms "so long as a piece of Plymouth Rock remained big enough to make a gunflint out of."[15]

In Massachusetts another anti-Catholic, anti-immigrant group, the Know Nothing Party, passed laws against Catholics and adopted the first statute requiring Bible reading in the schools.

Prayer in school became increasingly "nonsectarian" and voluntary to avoid such conflicts and controversies. To further prevent disputes, most states allowing religious exercises such as Bible reading prohibited teachers from commenting on the text.

Even as the narrowly religious character of both public and private schools diminished, an argument was often made for a theistic commitment in education. In 1949 the International Council on Religious Education, now a division of the National

Council of Churches, declared that there ought to be education for theism in public schools. In 1950 the National Council of Independent Schools issued a statement on "The Function of Secondary Education in the United States," which recognized that separation of church and state forbade compulsory worship and protected the rights of dissent, but still insisted that "the reliance on God and trust in Him . . . were to be recognized and perpetuated." There is a "spiritual heritage to which our children are entitled," the statement read, which consists of a recognition that "our ultimate security and unity rests in an understanding of man's position in relation to eternal reality."[16]

THE INEVITABLE CIRCLE

But what of the moral dimension to education?

Most would agree that issues of values inevitably touch issues of morality, which are in turn linked by tradition and certification to religion. I have already noted that issues such as values clarification and sex education raise the central question of the role of education in fostering moral development. If the schools attempt to teach no values, they are open to the charge that an education devoid of values is not a genuine education at all, certainly not one worthy of the support of the state.

But since education must relate to character and the school has to introduce values into the educational program in a direct way, the question becomes: "What values?" From what sources shall they be derived? The values of the community? Of the teacher? Of state educational authorities? And if some moral rules are taught, how can they be justified? The "consensus" of society? The power and authority of "leaders"? Or are the rules inherently right? If so, we are back to religion again, aren't we?! It seems to be an inevitable circle.

BATTLE FOR THE PUBLIC SCHOOLS

Many observers are deeply critical of educators' tendency to ignore issues of values, or, when they do address them, to reject the family values of our national life. Tim LaHaye, in *The Battle for the Mind*, speaks of the humanists "brain washing . . . children under the guise of public education."

Nor are all educators disagreeing. "Anti-humanists do have a point that humanism, like traditional religions, does involve itself in morality and other value judgments," says Nicholas F.

Gier, professor of philosophy at the University of Idaho, in *Free Inquiry,* a humanist publication. "Furthermore, there is no question that basic humanistic values are part of our public school education."[17]

Gier admits that humanism may well be our civil religion and "an essential part of our American heritage." And Leo Pfeffer, premier church-state separationist, has himself described the "triumphs of secularism" in the struggle with religion in the public schools.

Terry Eastland, writing in the *Wall Street Journal*, also acknowledges the absence of moral education in schools, noting that when prayer and devotional exercises were barred from the schools, educators and sociologists, not the courts, introduced the "more sweeping idea that the public schools should teach everything but religion and morality." The result is that there are few instances of real moral education, and "the craze in the schools today is a type of moral 'education' that is unfortunately empty of substantive morality." The result is that "if young Americans are shaped, they are unfortunately shaped to be moral neuters," lacking the basic core of principles with which to deal with the genuine moral issues facing modern society.[18]

"Far more than daily prayer is needed," Eastland declares, "given the 'values-free' state of much of public education today. Everyone interested in the public schools should begin reviewing what is taught or failing to be taught in their schools, with a view toward making sure that the basic morality is recovered and instilled in the latest generation of students. Concerned teachers can make a difference here, but often the job will fall to parents, who are usually the least susceptible to educational fads like 'values clarification.' "[19]

Even the Supreme Court justices are beginning to worry about our current educational system. Chief Justice Burger complained in a speech in 1981 that "we have virtually eliminated from public schools . . . any effort to teach values of integrity, truth, personal accountability and respect for others' rights."

Terry Eastland is right: Far more than daily prayer is needed to fill the wasteland of American education. Certainly he raises a challenge to all of us to become involved, to investigate what is being taught in schools, and to try to challenge any humanistic indoctrination. We may be in a "battle for the public school," as Tim LaHaye suggests in his book of that title.

Certainly educators who advocate values clarification and other new programs are preparing to defend their philosophy. Sidney Simon, author of many values clarification textbooks, is calling for support of a national Coalition for Democracy in Education, an organization he is founding. He and noted psychologists Carl Rogers and Lawrence Kohlberg ask all others who are worried about current attacks on humanistic education and values clarification to join them. Simon notes the threats of censorship, prayer, and creation, and says he has established a "crisis hotline."

His letter quotes a statement from the July 6 issue of *Newsweek*. "The Moral Majority's war on secular humanism threatens to become as virulent as the witch hunts of the 50s."

But who is doing more damage in America today, the so-called "witch hunters" or the "witches"? Let's hope all those involved in this "battle" will consider the American school children who may either benefit—or be injured—by the education they receive.

10

The Fly in the Ointment?

A Dr. Seuss classic begins:

> Every who
> Down in Who-ville
> Liked Christmas a lot . . .
> But the Grinch,
> Who lived just north of Who-ville,
> Did NOT!

"Dr. Seuss did not say so, but I am sure the Grinch was a member of the American Civil Liberties Union," complained George Will in a 1979 column in the *Washington Post*.

"Every December they crawl out of the woodwork," Will went on to observe. "Grinchy people who seem to live for the fun of trying to get Christmas trees, carols, and creches banned from public places. . . . These people want to use state power to purge the social milieu of certain things offensive, but not at all harmful, to them. There is a meanness, even bullying, in this—a disagreeable delight in using the community's law divisively, to abolish traditions enjoyed by neighbors."[1]

Legal counsels who argue for school prayer or the rights of Christian students notice the same adversary. It is likely that the counsel at the other table in the courtroom is from the ACLU. These initials have become disagreeable to many Christians. If you ask who has created the legal controversy over prayers like "God is great; God is good" or the rights of Christian students at campuses, many people will answer, "The ACLU!"

Certainly the American Civil Liberties Union is not a friend of the new right, although the ACLU has acknowledged an increase in membership of one-hundred thousand over the last years as they have taken a stand against conservative groups. The areas of contention? Abortion. Capital punishment. Homosexual rights. And of course, school prayer.

The confrontation has become so public that an ACLU ad in the *New York Times* declared: "If the Moral Majority has its Way, You'd Better Start Praying!" A sarcastic play on words, since the ad's sponsor has not been a vigorous proponent of prayer.

But others besides the new right are criticizing the ACLU. Lieutenant Mike Curb of California called the ACLU a "lobbying force for criminals," which is "constantly taking a position against the legitimate interests of law abiding citizens."[2] Indeed Curb insisted the ACLU was "taking advantage of our constitutional rights." Edwin Meese, top White House official and counselor to President Ronald Reagan called the ACLU the "criminal lobby."[3]

Controversy is not new to the ACLU. The organization thrives on it. In 1964, founder Roger Baldwin, far from timid at the age of eighty, still echoed the ACLU's feisty spirit: "I think highly of reformers, revolutionists, dreamers, dissenters, (and) disturbers of the status quo.[4] The list of clients the ACLU has represented shows that Baldwin (who directed the ACLU for its first three decades) was not whistling Dixie: real and alleged Communists, atheists and religious fanatics, union dissenters, controversial authors and publishers of pornographic materials, criminals, Nazis, prisoners, and the Ku Klux Klan. The ACLU has also represented teachers, religious groups, newspaper editors, parents, racial minorities, and others whose civil rights were being stepped on by government authority.

A 1977 case illustrates the ACLU's diverse commitment to civil liberties. The organization defended the rights of Nazi demonstrators to march in the strongly Jewish community of Skokie, Illinois. The march was deliberately provocative and insulting to many residents who still bore the marks of German prison camps. But faithful to its multifaceted commitment to free speech, the ACLU declared that the Nazis had the same freedom to march and speak that our Constitution guarantees to

all groups. The case cost the ACLU thousands of members.
Perhaps a third of its Illinois constituents resigned in protest.

WHAT IS THE ACLU?

The ACLU is a national organization with numerous local
affiliates; the total membership is about three-hundred thousand
and includes over five thousand attorneys who provide their services, largely without fee, to the causes championed by the
organization.

The ACLU is most noted for taking legal action to represent clients on issues of civil liberties or filing arguments with
courts to set forth its opinion on issues others have brought to
trial. But in addition the ACLU engages in significant public
education projects, and frequently testifies before federal and
state government committees on proposed legislation. Its
publishing includes a rather excellent series of handbooks on the
rights of various groups of citizens, including teachers,
prisoners, parents, older persons, the poor, tenants, physically
handicapped persons, and homosexuals.

But sensational cases give the ACLU its image. Look at the
following list of causes championed by the ACLU:

- Challenged a 1962 statute that allowed the
  Post Office Department to detain communist
  propaganda.
- Opposed the Connecticut ban on contracep-
  tives.
- Challenged a state university regulation that
  prohibited students from living in a Christian
  "fraternity" but allowed them to live in other
  group homes.
- Defended the rights of the parents of Walter
  Polovchak, the thirteen-year-old boy who
  wanted to stay in the United States when his
  parents decided to go back to their home in the
  Soviet Union.
- Challenged the validity of juries from which
  blacks had been systematically excluded.
- Challenged the Arkansas 1981 law providing
  for equal time for teaching creation in the
  public schools.

- Defended the right of a California woman to put a Goldwater placard in her yard, in defiance of a local ordinance that banned political signs on residential property.
- Challenged police practices that allow police to strip-search women charged with minor traffic violations.
- Challenged a Louisiana law forbidding crimes against nature.

It's a mixed lot, isn't it? But all the suits promote individual freedom against some kind of government regulation: religious, moral, or political.

ROGER BALDWIN AND THE ACLU

In January of 1981, Roger Baldwin, then ninety-six years old, received the Presidential Medal of Freedom, the nation's highest honor, from William J. Vanden Heuvel, United States deputy ambassador to the United Nations. He declared that the "Constitution of the United States in important measure has endured and thrived because Roger Baldwin and the ACLU have been its champion, its defender and its guardian." And Walter Cronkite said Baldwin's achievements caused others who have received the award to "pale in significance." President Jimmy Carter called him a "national resource . . . an inspiration . . . a saint."

Baldwin came from a moderately well-to-do Massachusetts family and bore the credentials of his upper middle-class heritage. He attended Harvard, and while there showed his sympathies for the unfortunate by organizing his fellow students as tutors of underprivileged children. After college he went to St. Louis where he managed a settlement house and became chief probation officer for the St. Louis Juvenile Court. The rebel in him was always evident. In 1912 he led a protest because Margaret Sanger was unable to rent a hall for a lecture on birth control, and another protest because police refused to allow unemployed persons to meet on the steps of the Old Court House.

The American Civil Liberties Union evolved from Baldwin's interest in the labor movement and his opposition to the First World War. In 1916 Baldwin joined a St. Louis chapter of the American Union Against Militarism (AUAM), a group opposed to United States participation in the European war. Soon he was involved in a subdivision, the Bureau for Conscientious Objectors, a cause that was so distasteful to the public and some AUAM members that its name was changed to the Civil Liberties Bureau.

The group defended C.O.'s and pacifists and persons prosecuted under the Espionage Acts. It also opposed widespread censorship of the mail, which resulted from wartime fear and hysteria. These activities were mild compared to protests during the Vietnam period; but to an earlier America, the bureau seemed radical. America brooked no opposition to the war. Some dissenters were forced to kiss the flag in public. Sixty-four were tarred and feathered, and fifty-five kidnapped and whipped. Criminal penalities were also severe in some cases: sentences of fifteen years for talking against the draft, ten years for opposing Liberty Loans, and twenty years for calling the government a liar and predicting a German victory. For civil libertarians this was a violation of the Constitution's First Amendment.

Opposition to the conscientious objector issue became so heated within the AUAM that the Civil Liberties Bureau finally split off from the organization and again assumed a new name, this time the National Civil Liberties Bureau with Baldwin as the director and noted socialist Norman Thomas as vice-president.

On August 31, 1918, the bureau offices were raided by FBI officials and members of the Union League Club. Only twelve days later, Roger was called to register for the draft and responded by writing to the Draft Board. "I will decline to perform any service under compulsion . . ."[5] In a letter to the New York attorney general, he went further in explaining his views, indicating he would not seek to avoid the penalties. "I do not seek martyrdom. I desire no public notoriety. . . . All I ask of you is a speedy trial. I shall of course plead guilty."

On October 30, 1918, his trial was held. When Baldwin testified, he openly proposed a radically different world order. "I share the extreme radical philosophy of the future society. I look forward to a social order without any external restraints upon the individual."[6]

The judge noted that "he who disobeys the law . . . must, as you are prepared to—take the consequences" and sentenced

Baldwin to prison where he served ten months and eleven days.

The year after he was released, Baldwin formed the ACLU during a final reorganization of the National Civil Liberties Bureau. The first board of the ACLU included sixty-four persons, among them religious leaders like Dr. Harry F. Ward of Union Theological Seminary in New York; labor leaders like Duncan MacDonald, president of the United Mine Workers in Chicago; notables like Helen Keller and Jane Addams; James Weldon of the National Association for the Advancement of Colored People (NAACP); William Z. Foster, a radical labor leader; and Felix Frankfurter who was to become a justice of the United States Supreme Court.

But the key was Baldwin.

His idealistic spirit and sympathies were clearly with the left. In 1920 he was instrumental in forming the Mutual Aid Society, an organization he said was made up of "leftist intellectuals, trade unionists, the radical fringe" to provide aid for a variety of leftist persons.

In the introduction to *Letters from Russian Prisons*, he wrote about communism. "Many of the members of the Committee for Political Prisoners [a group of which he was a member] . . . regard the Russian Revolution as the greatest and most daring experiment yet undertaken to create society in terms of human values."[7]

In 1927 he was commissioned by Vanguard Press to write a monograph on liberty in the Soviet Union. That June he visited the Soviet Union, but his bias was again evident as he wrote the monograph. "Repressions in Soviet Russia are weapons of struggle in a transition period to socialism. The society the Communists seek to create will be freed of class struggle—if achieved—and therefore of repression."[8] A close friend of Baldwin's, Emma Goldman, wrote to him condemning his attitude toward the evils in the Soviet Union. "People as naive as you are hopeless," she chided.

But Baldwin's leftist bent continued. In 1934 he wrote an article in *Soviet Russia Today* entitled "Freedom in the USA." "I too take a class position," he said. "It is anti-capitalist and pro-revolutionary. . . . I champion civil liberty as the best of the non-violent means of building the power on which the worker's rule must be based. If I aid the reactionaries to get free speech now and then . . . it is only because those liberties help to create a more hospitable atmosphere for working-class liberties. The class struggle is the central conflict of the world; all others are incidental. . . . When that power of the working class is once achieved, as it has been only in the Soviet Union, I am for maintaining it by any means whatever."[9]

In 1935 he answered a questionnaire for the thirtieth reunion of his Harvard class with the flamboyant statement, "Communism is our goal."

Baldwin also continued his involvement in the United Fronts: the League Against Imperialism, the League Against War and Facism (which became the League for Peace and Democracy), and the Spanish Refugee Relief Campaign. Later he acknowledged that the Communists had lied when they said that the leaders of the United Fronts were not party members. But Baldwin was not fooled, even at this time. In 1972 he admitted to an interviewer, "I knew what I was doing; I was not the innocent liberal, and I was not a fellow traveler either."

Later Roger Baldwin regretted some of his earlier communist leanings. He admitted to reporters that his earlier prejudices had blinded him to clear signs of the truth. "I went on making allowances for what I should, in my own mind at least, have condemned and rejected."[10]

"I always thought communism and socialism were good ideas, but as Nehru once said about them, 'They're great ideas, but when attached to the machinery of a police state, man must be against them.' So . . . I don't want Communists around here."[11]

While the radicalism of much of Baldwin's life was never the official policy of the ACLU, it undoubtedly colored the character of this organization, which Baldwin dominated until 1950.

THE ACLU v. RELIGION?

The ACLU's suits on religious issues began in 1927 when the organization undertook the defense of Warner Williams, who had been convicted and sentenced to six months for writing a book that contained the sentence "Jesus Christ was immoral." Later, in 1931, the ACLU challenged a New York practice that prevented atheistic street meetings.

The ACLU has at times represented and defended religious believers against government challenges, although these cases have often been at the initiative of a local chapter and may not have expressed the policy of national officials. In the 1970s a local ACLU organization successfully defended a group of Christian students at the University of Delaware (*Keegan* v. *Delaware*). These students wished to meet in the lounge of their dormitory for religious worship, but university officials refused, declaring that this was prohibited by the Establishment Clause of the Constitution. The rights of the students were upheld.

In an Illinois case, the local ACLU represented a group of Christian freshmen who sought to live in off-campus housing like freshman sorority and fraternity members. The university refused, and the ACLU challenged the discrimination against religious students. (However, the university eliminated the bias by changing its policy to restrict all freshmen from living in off-campus housing units.)

On many occasions, the ACLU has represented generally unpopular religious groups. For example in 1943 they published a thirty-six page pamphlet explaining the Jehovah's Witnesses' position on military service. But more often the ACLU has been the opponent in lawsuits involving religious practices.

In April of 1981 the Pittsburgh chapter of the ACLU sought an injunction to prevent a full-time religious channel from broadcasting on cable television, charging that this was an unconstitutional violation of separation of church and state.

The suit was filed on behalf of the Reverend Jesse Cavileer, minister of the Allegheny Center Unitarian Church, Joseph Houle, minister of the Metropolitan Community Church of Oakland (a church composed mainly of homosexuals), and Samuel Lane of Brookline, a member of the American Atheists.

ACLU groups have attacked local school policies that allowed religious students to have the same right to meet before school that other students have (such as the *Lubbock* case in which the local affiliate, Lubbock Civil Liberties Union, challenged the school board). The ACLU has also defended university policies that discriminated against religious students by limiting the number of times they could meet in university facilities (*Dittman* v. *Western Washington University*). And, as George Will noted in his "The Grinch Who Stole Christmas" article, the ACLU has opposed the right of schools to utilize music with religious as well as cultural significance in holiday programs (*Florey* v. *Sioux Falls*). They are well known for their frequent complaints about any school prayers, Christmas celebrations, and creches.

The basis of the ACLU's frequent challenges of religion in public life is a seemingly myopic view of the Religion Clause of the First Amendment, which emphasizes the "wall of separation" between church and state. This view seeks to search out—and then root out of public institutions—religious practices, however long standing, however voluntary, however minimal. They have become crusaders for a religious wasteland.

ARE THEY THE ENEMY?

No! As much as I oppose certain policies and postures of the ACLU and often find myself on the opposite side on issues of religious liberty, there are many ways in which the ACLU's overall perspective is proper. At times they have protected the tradition of liberty in which we all thrive. We need people who will speak for the rights of the underdog, even when that person or group holds ideas we find repulsive and offensive. As Harry Boer writes in the *Reformed Journal*: the ACLU has "established itself as a formidable fighter for liberty." When the ACLU opposes a government action in Virginia that would have allowed involuntary sterilization of psychiatric patients, they are developing precedents that assure freedom from the government intrusion of George Orwell's *1984* for all of us.

As a minority people, who ought to know how fragile community and liberty is, Christians ought to be thankful for the scope of freedoms in our country. Rights of minorities gained today by unpopular, even reprehensible, persons may well be the basis for our freedoms in the future. In fact, Christians ought to be embarrassed by their own failure to speak for liberty and freedom. It is not necessary to agree with the ACLU on every individual case or issue to appreciate that they are a powerful force for liberty.

BUT!

Nevertheless, there are areas where the ACLU has done a disservice to freedom or evidences "inconsistency, pettiness, questionable judgment, and mere show of power," as Harry Boer noted in the *Reformed Journal*.

In the area of religious liberty, the ACLU has seemed to take an extreme posture in its commitment to separation. Frank

Sorauf in *Wall of Separation* observes the extensive role of the ACLU in the major cases that have established the "separationist" concept. He indicates that this separationist perspective comes in part from the "agnosticism and militant atheism" of ACLU members and in part from a secular humanist perspective, which is "skeptical and free thinking." These elements create a "separationism tied closely to the rejection of dogmatic and authoritative religion."[12]

Though the American Civil Liberties Union would no doubt deny it—and point to the members of the clergy in their constituency—there is a bias in the ACLU against religion in many of its public expressions, especially religion that is dogmatic. What else can account for their desire to deny students at universities and high schools the right to meet and discuss religion? If the students wished to discuss other concepts—or form an ACLU group—civil libertarians would rush to their defense. But they oppose religious groups. It is a bias seen in the *McLean* v. *Arkansas* case, in which the ACLU challenged a statute providing for equal treatment of creation science. While there is nothing amiss in their legal right to represent the opponents, it is revealing that a concurrent ACLU fundraising event included a party spoofing the entire interest in creation and purposely belittling and ridiculing creation science.

The ACLU is a strong defender of abortion rights, but when does it represent the rights of the unborn? No longer does the ACLU simply defend those who come and seek its aid, the organization seems to have a mission, apparently seeking clients to challenge certain issues. This bias may be largely unconscious, emerging from a combination of the ACLU's history and its current constituency, but it is a bias, one that is unbecoming to a body that purports to speak for freedom and liberty.

I am also concerned about the tendency of the ACLU to use its influence and power to intimidate public officials. The organization may or may not plan to do so, but its actions have that effect. There is, of course, nothing wrong in pressing persons to obey the law. But often groups such as the ACLU press persons to accept their interpretation of the law, which is determined by their underlying ideology—an ideology that is not without prejudice.

How would the public react if the Moral Majority sent a letter to school districts throughout a state, insisting that they advise the Moral Majority of school practices regarding religion and demanding that certain documents be produced? The press, the public, and the ACLU would be outraged. Yet the ACLU sent a letter to school officials in the state of Washington that read:

This is a request for copies of certain documents pursuant to the Washington Public Disclosure Act, R.C.V. 42,17 etsaq.

The ACLU of Washington requests copies of the following documents:

1. Any statement of policy, or staff instructions, operating procedures, manuals or directives regarding the separation of church and state, the involvement of religion in schools, the use of property for religious instruction, activity or worship and the teaching of religion or the Bible in schools.
2. Announcements and/or programs for the December holiday, for Christmas assemblies or services for the last five years.
3. Announcements and/or programs for any Baccalaureate services for the last five years.
4. The syllabus and reading lists of any courses in which the Bible and religion are taught.
5. The syllabus of any portion in which "creation" is taught as an alternative to evolution.
6. Announcements or programs for any Easter assembly or service for the last five years.
7. Any documents that disclose practices concerning student, teacher or staff prayers occurring on school property.
8. Any documents concerning the practices or activities of students' religious groups on school property.

As you are aware, the Public Disclosure Act requires that responses to requests for public records shall be made promptly by agencies.

Any denial must be accompanied by a written
statement of the specific grievance for denial.

While the practices of public schools must be available to
the public and, therefore, the ACLU has a right to such information, the process reflects the organization's tendency to see
itself as a crusader to root out the impermissible. Such practices
tend to intimidate school officials into avoiding even permissible
aspects of religious involvement in public schools.

A final area of concern is more philosophic: the apparent
inability of the ACLU to perceive any significant limits on individual liberties. I feel this blinds them to the importance of
culture and public morality. The ACLU has become one of the
most influential legal defenders of obscenity and pornography in
the nation. Playboy Foundation is a significant contributor to
various ACLU causes, and, in fact, National ACLU Secretary
Franklyn Halman received the Playboy Foundation's First
Amendment Award in 1982.

The ACLU's commitment to liberty is impressive and fundamental, but it is difficult to perceive how the practices of
Penthouse and *Hustler* are related to the fundamental commitments of free speech intended by the writers of the First
Amendment. An exaggerated notion of individual freedom may
finally destroy a society.

Boer points to an illustrative case, the ACLU's suit to
eliminate the self-policing regulations of the film industry. The
ACLU challenged the right of theaters to prevent children from
viewing R- and X-rated movies, claiming the system "inhibits
freedom of expression." The complaining party was a prominent member of an ACLU national committee, not a child who
ran to the ACLU offices to seek help. What constitutional rights
were really being violated? What danger to society existed in the
local theater's policies? Suits such as these illustrate a
"trivialization" and a myopic perspective on the nature and
character of rights in any society.

I believe one must defend civil rights with the ACLU's vigor
and commitment. And I believe we should recognize that such
efforts may frequently place an organization in the position of
defending the most unlovely persons, because that is where our
commitments to liberty are most clearly tested. Therefore, many
of the criticisms directed at the ACLU for their defenses of

criminals, Nazis, and leftists are shortsighted.

But I do not agree with the ACLU's theory of separation of church and state or its inability to distinguish free speech and press from filth. On these points, it is our right, and our duty, to reject the ACLU's crusade.

11

God and Country—Still Partners?

In 1824 Andrew Jackson, then the U.S. senator from Tennessee, described this country as "manifestly called by the Almighty to a destiny which Greece and Rome, in the days of their pride, might have envied." Jackson's idea was shortened in later years by other politicians to the words *manifest destiny*, a term referring to the United States' mission in the world under God.

God and country. Many Americans feel the United States has been used by God and blessed by God because of its devotion to God. How will the erosion of such public observances as school prayer affect the nation's future, they wonder. Will blessing turn to curse? On the other hand, are there dangers to using religious activities for political purposes?

"If we ignore the compulsion which comes from the hearts of the people concerning [school prayer], we will be put in the position of throwing the switch which connects a central dynamo to the light of this great nation." So Congressman Frank Becker argued before Congress. Many in America still believe that God is essential to our national life. Seven Princeton professors issued "The Spiritual Basis of Democracy" in 1942, a statement "arguing that democratic principles must be grounded in religious principles."[1]

"We are not talking about religion. We are talking about God," said Martha Roundtree of the Leadership Foundation as she warned of the dangers of abolishing God from American public life. And of course, Justice William Douglas did say that we are a religious people "whose institutions presuppose a Supreme Being."

Thomas Jefferson, who gets quoted by all sides, seemed to see a necessary connection between freedom and the belief in a Supreme Being. "God, Who gave us life, gave us liberty. Can the liberties of a nation be secure when we have removed a conviction that these liberties are the gift of God?"[2]

What is the relationship between prayer in schools, or other national symbols of faith, and national success? Law professor Charles Rice, in his volume on the school prayer issue (written in the sixties), noted the "world struggle for liberty"—a conflict he said was filled with "spiritual dimensions." In that struggle it is essential, Rice declared, that there be an affirmation that the "rights of man are derived from God." He decried the Supreme Court's rulings, which appear to "fasten an agnostic orthodoxy upon the government of the U.S."[3]

Many compare the effects of the Court decisions with the official position of the Soviet Union. They note the Soviet Constitution, which specifically provides that the church shall be separate from the school and vows an atheistic posture. It is, these observers claim, the spiritual character of American society that distinguishes it from communism and its materialistic perspective. John Sparkman, former senator from Alabama, noting Soviet separation of church and state, said, "I look with disfavor on a step that draws us closer to that concept."[4]

Is the American way of life, with its democratic and republican principles of the rights of man, based on a Judeo-Christian tradition? Is that tradition essential for its maintenance? And is school prayer an important element in fostering that ethic? These are not simple questions, for they touch issues of historical interpretation, philosophy, and theology.

VALUES: A BASE FOR DEMOCRACY

It does seem clear that the Judeo-Christian tradition and democracy are far from inevitably related, for as historian Sidney Hook rightly observes, our religion vastly predates democracy. In fact, during most of Christianity's history, democracy was unknown. The principles of Christianity were as likely to be used to support the divine right of kings as any other political philosophy. Even though Christians held to certain doctrines of man's equality before God, they tragically did not act this out in political terms.

Nor is heaven a democracy, as Hook notes. "Whatever the political organization of Heaven may be, it certainly does not suggest a democratic republic."[5]

In theory a thoroughly secular state could elect to govern itself by democratic principles. But no government may long function without deciding the critical issues of the legitimate role of government as it competes with the individual and other units of society, such as the family and the church. Neither can government function without developing some sense of values and norms. By what shall it judge its actions? By what standard shall its courts or police function?

In this encounter with issues of power and justice, a government is likely to become a tyranny administered by whoever has the guns and dollars—unless it has a concept of law above and beyond itself. If there are no truths, how can anyone call the government—or even the citizens—to account? God's truth, even more than a constitution, will protect man from his baser moments.

In this sense, government must have some conscious or unconscious values and standards. If it has none, sheer power rules. As Bishop James Pike observed in criticizing the Supreme Court's decisions, there must be a standard of right and wrong and a "recognition of dependence upon Almighty God and of the fact that He is the highest reality, not the state." This recognition is contained in the Declaration of Independence, where the rights of man are "endowed by their Creator." There are realms beyond the state's legitimate powers, inherent rights not delegated by the state.

Indeed in a culture where government has such massive power in the form of technology, taxation, and regulation, the power of the state is a moral issue. What shall be the limits of that power? Not laws alone, not even constitutions can check this power, unless those institutions have the weight of moral force behind them. Congressman Philip Crane (R-Ill.), in an interview in *U.S. News and World Report*, warned that when nations reject a Supreme Being they have "turned to the alternative of unlimited power vested in a secular state."[6]

J. Paul Williams, writing in "The Schoolmen and

Religion," makes a similar point, claiming that while religious indoctrination should not be at pub'ic expense, there are certain areas in which "religion must be public, the concern of all . . . these are basic ethical propositions on which society is founded. Unless these ethical propositions attain the level of religious conviction, they lack staying power and society is endangered."[7]

Perhaps the most striking case of power coming under the rule of law was the Watergate investigation of 1973 and 1974, an investigation that reached even the nation's chief executive. During the proceedings, the Supreme Court ruled that President Richard M. Nixon could not use any "executive privilege" to dodge Special Prosecutor Leon Jaworski's subpoena of the tapes critical to the investigation. Said Jaworski later, "During the ordeal, it [the Constitution] was interpreted again to reaffirm the truth that no one—absolutely no one—is above the law." In this, the Constitution was reflecting a higher moral standard.

Yet Jaworski realized that the Constitution and the law would have been powerless had not individual men had the moral fortitude to enforce them. In his autobiography *Crossroads*, he speculated:

> Suppose these individuals and courts had not measured up courageously and judiciously to the traumatic issues? . . .
>
> Nothing surprised me more than the attitude of a segment of citizens who could not be bothered by the revelations of [Watergate]. With a wave of their arm or a shrug of the shoulders, they would remark, "It has been going on for a long time." Or, "It did not begin with Watergate."
>
> How long these practices may have been going on—or whether such perfidy was greater or lesser or equal to Watergate—is not even a mitigating circumstance. The question is: Why were these instances not brought to light? Why were the offenders not called to an accounting for their wrongs?
>
> The answer would have to be that they were condoned.[8]

Religion and morals are necessary ingredients of a successful democracy. But the fact that society needs an informing ethic does not mean that school prayers ought to be organized activities of the state. There is a difference between the essential requirements for a society and government's involvement in those activities. Many advocates of school prayer arranged by the government are opponents of government interference in private affairs. All that a society needs cannot be arranged by government. And even if it could be, it would not necessarily be desirable.

Society needs a faith and a morality. But it is dangerous for government to develop that faith; it may be like the fox guarding the hen house. You then have the dangerous potential of a religious system created by government to support its own abuses. Such a system occurred in Nazi Germany in the 1930s and 1940s, when many Germans referred to themselves as *Gottglaubige*. Reinhold Kerstan, who had been a member of the Hitler Youth during World War II, writes that the *Gottglaubige* "was a term the Nazis had invented and literally meant 'believers in God.' But it referred to the gods of Germanic origin, not to the God of the Bible. The *Gottglaubigen* believed in the state and the mystical religion of a super race."[9]

Perhaps you agree that government ought to stay out of morality and spiritual development. But whose task is it then? Certainly it is the home's. And the church's. But what about the schools, which consume so much of a child's life? Shouldn't the religious element be there? This is where theory clashes with practice. Education surely is one place where the underpinnings of a moral system ought to be taught. But in our government-supported system and our pluralistic society, the content of moral education is difficult to determine. What would school prayer do for this education? Probably very little. There's an oft-told tale about a young urban child who, in the days of the Lord's Prayer recitation in the classroom, prayed, ". . . And lead us not into Penn Station. . . ."

Somehow he'd missed the point!

PRAYER WITH A POLITICAL PURPOSE

Prayer's "objective is to make good men and good citizens. . . . School prayer is an extension of the political tradition," declared Alfred Balitzer, writing for the Moral Majority Report.

School prayer serves not a religious purpose at all, but a political purpose, he claimed. The argument that prayer has a political purpose is a major reason why some with deep religious convictions oppose school and government involvement in prayer.

Whenever a variety of religious traditions are involved in government-sanctioned prayer, the result is likely to be what Americans United for Separation of Church and State called "an empty salute to religion." The trend was evident in the Regents' Prayer, which had little substance. Is such an allegedly "nonsectarian," "stretch sock" kind of prayer good for society? Good for religion?

Advocates of school prayer in the days before the initial Supreme Court decisions hailed the "nonsectarian" character of the prayers, claiming they helped teach a reliance on God and exemplified the common Judeo-Christian faith. Somehow a prayer could be written to please everyone, they hoped, or nearly so. But as someone observed, "history is not encouraging" to those who seek such a prayer.[10] In 1962, Bishop Fulton J. Sheen suggested one idea to Congressman Peter Rodino in debates about the Becker Amendment. "Every member of Congress is already carrying [a prayer] with him in his pocket—'In God we Trust.' "

"Is that all?" Rodino asked, incredulously.[11]

Such empty prayers soon lose all religious meaning. Indeed the Supreme Court has upheld prayers in Congress and such statements on our coins by claiming they are not religious but "mere commemoration of a historical fact" (as Justice Brennan said in *Schempp*). What a tragic admission of the emptiness of political prayer! It's like the judgment of a New Jersey court, which upheld invocations at city council meetings because there was nothing especially religious about invocations. They did help, the court declared, "solemnify" the occasion.

Some advocates of school prayer use similar logic today, contending that even if such prayers are not profound theological statements, they are important symbols of a higher order. They bear witness to our historic reliance on God, and invite the pupils to recognize this element in our public life.

Rabbi Polish of the Synagogue Council of America disagrees: "I am an advocate of sectarianism." If prayer is truly nonsectarian, it will "trivialize the nature of prayer itself." It will tend to diminish rather than enhance the importance of prayer for those who are forced to participate. What you will have, Polish concluded, is a "secular religion, a religion of the state."

W. Hubert Porter, an American Baptist, declared that there is little resemblance between school prayer and biblical prayer. Unlike school prayer, "Biblical prayer is never very far from the Lamb slain from the foundation of the world."[12]

Senator John Danforth (R-Mo.), an Episcopal priest, was right when he declared that "for those within a religious tradition, it simply is not true that one prayer is as good as any other. "True prayer," he noted, "is robust prayer. It is bold prayer. It is almost by definition sectarian prayer."[13]

"A homogenized religious recitation, perfunctorily rendered by children who have just tumbled from a bus or playground, is not apt to arise from the individual wills, as real prayer must," wrote George Will in *Newsweek*.[14] Will warns against "instant religiosity" as a bland substitute comparable to processed cheese and instant mashed potatoes.

Many have pointed to their own past experiences with school prayers that were empty of spiritual content. This emptiness, they recall, was a combination of teachers whose spiritual commitment to the process was lacking and the charade these exercises became for students. *Liberty* magazine carried the story of Rabbi Leo Trepp, who grew up in Germany where prayer was required at the beginning of school; students were divided into different groups according to their religious traditions. Some teachers resisted the whole process; students made a mockery of it. Sometimes students would intentionally start to use the long form of prayer, and then a teacher would bang the desk and demand the short one be used. Others insisted that the prayer begin as the teacher entered the room and be completed by the time the teacher reached the desk. "Where was the result, the conviction, the spirit, the courage?" Rabbi Trepp asks. "How many parents may have eased their conscience by saying: I need do nothing or little in religious education for my children: the state takes care of that?"

"I believe the future of our nation depends on the religious education we give our children—an education that will take root at home and church or synagogue, in full and free commitment to the word and mandate of God," the rabbi concluded.[15]

Miriam Stoyer Thomas, a teacher in the South Harpswell,

Maine, school system, wrote a letter to the editor of the *Christian Science Monitor*, describing her experiences with school prayer:

> The people who advocate the Lord's Prayer in public schools should be there just once and hear it. 20,000 times in my life I have heard the following: 1,200 to 2,000 noisy teenagers shuffle in and get seated. Some unknown, five flights down in the school office, mumbles as fast as possible: "And the menu today is sloppy Joes and m-m-m (unintelligible) apples. And the football game tonight m-m-m-m- Our Father who art in Heaven . . . blankety, blankety, Hallowed be thy name. . . . Make ups will be Thursday in the gym . . . forgive us our debts. . . . Ice cream for sale. Get your tickets. Amen."
>
> Now if Sen. Jesse Helms or some other legislator thinks THAT adds to good Christian or Buddhist or Hindu living, let him explain.[16]

John Warwick Mongomery, dean of the Simon Greenleaf School of Law and a noted theologian, seems to concur with these criticisms of school-structured prayer. Writing in *Christianity Today*, Montgomery noted that his objection is primarily theological. He notes an example of school prayer that was suggested to Senator Jesse Helms during a Senate debate about his prayer bill in 1981:

> Senator John C. Danforth (R-Mo.) asked of Helms: "Let us assume that a teacher of, say third-grade students, is a very devout Roman Catholic, and she goes into class one day and writes on the blackboard behind her desk the words of the 'Hail Mary.' She then announces, 'Children, we will now have a voluntary recitation of this prayer. Those of you who do not want to recite it, need not recite it; those of you who wish to, please join with me.' Would it be the Senator's view that the Department of

Justice, in such a case, should not go into court and a court should not entertain such a case?"

Helms replied: "I say to the Senator that the scenario he has concocted does not bother me at all. I am a Baptist. I would not object at all to my grandchildren being in a class where that happened, and I do not think the majority of the American people would." Pressed as to whether he would feel the same way if he were an orthodox Jew, Helms said that he would.

We find it remarkable that Danforth's very realistic "scenario" did not "bother" Helms "at all." Theologically, it *ought* to bother evangelical, Bible-believing Christians very much indeed. The Bible insists on prayers *in the name of Jesus* (John 14:13-14; Col. 3:17). Thus, in the voluntary prayer atmosphere Senator Helms is promoting, Christian children would have to be instructed by their parents and their pastors not to participate whenever school prayers were biblically unjustifiable. This would, of course, apply also to "Hail Marys" since "there is *one* mediator between God and men, the man Christ Jesus" (1 Tim. 2:5).[17]

Clearly Danforth and Montgomery have identified a critical problem with school prayers in today's environment. As Montgomery notes, the prayers in Boston might well be Unitarian, those in Utah, Mormon, and in San Francisco, perhaps directed to Vishnu or even LaVey's Satan.

Mongomery further complains that such exercises rob minority children and their parents "from a free decision for Christ. Evangelism thrives on true freedom and is crushed by social conformity."

I am amazed that the very persons who lament the basic secularism of teachers and educators want to enlist those same educators to monitor school prayer times! Can you imagine the sarcasm and innuendo that might accompany some school prayers? Many of us would just as soon leave prayer to those who truly wish to engage in it. Those who truly seek the Lord might not want to stay within the one- or five-minute limit. They will want more than "weak tea" or an outward show of religion. Prayer must be more than a political tool.

PART THREE
A FEW REBUTTALS

12

The Verdict
On School Prayer

It sounds almost un-American and suspiciously "liberal," if not downright subversive, to be against school prayer. After all, education is inextricably caught up with religious issues. Our founding fathers endorsed prayer. It's an important symbol of our accountability to God, and people can be excused if they don't like it. What more could you want?

I join with people whose conservative credentials are impeccable—people like John Warwick Montgomery of the Simon Greenleaf School of Law and C. Donald Cole of Moody Bible Institute—in being suspicious of officially organized school prayer. I don't reject it because it would be terrible—but because the prayers would be inadequate. I reject them not primarily on legal or constitutional grounds (the amendment would solve the constitutional question anyway, since you can't have an unconstitutional constitutional amendment), and certainly not on historical grounds. My reluctance is based primarily on religious and spiritual premises. Many of my reasons have already been indicated by implication, but allow me to state them specifically now.

Official, school-organized prayer times will almost surely fall short of a biblical vision of prayer as confession, petition, intercession, praise, and thanksgiving. Such whistlestop prayers are poor lessons for students about what prayer means. Prayer is too sacred to be secularized or used as a political tool.

It is surprising that evangelicals and fundamentalists have become so easily drafted into the school prayer campaign. Of all religious groups, they ought to recognize the deeply spiritual character of prayer and reject secular forms of pseudo-piety. Of all people, they ought to perceive the more basic ills in society and education, and know that a ritual, however symbolic, does not touch the root of the problem. School-administered prayer may very easily become "solemn assemblies," which the prophet Amos described as a hated "noise" to God when there is not concurrent righteousness and justice. When the wellsprings of faith are there, the ritual or symbol will give witness to it. But when the substance is gone, it is an illusion, like the religious rituals Amos condemned in Israel.

We also run the risk that school-organized prayers will be "used" by teachers or other government entities in ways that interfere with their spiritual character. Roger Williams was right when he insisted that there is a wall placed between the church and the state to keep the wilderness of the state from invading and destroying the garden of the church.

Despite the Supreme Court decision in *Engel*, state-written prayers (that nondenominational milk-toast I previously mentioned) may not be too far away. A White House briefing paper on the president's amendment declared: "If groups of people are to be permitted prayer, someone must have the power to determine the content of such prayers."

Even more than bland, meaningless prayer, I fear the cacophony and confusion that could develop in the schools of our nation if another option is used: that of a moment of meditation. Imagine a Krishna devotee chanting in one corner of the room, someone meditating in the lotus position in another corner, several Protestants reciting the Lord's Prayer, Jewish students intoning the *shema*. . . .

Pluralism is not only common among students. More critically, perhaps, pluralism is common among many teachers and administrative personnel who would show little sympathy for and perhaps even hostility to prayer. We do not need thoroughgoing secularists running prayer times in our schools.

There certainly are communities within the United States where there is a general religious consensus. In such communities, school prayers are perhaps still conducted even now. In such environments, the saying of grace over lunch in the elementary classroom may seem quite natural. Children and parents may well expect it. And frankly, it does seem that in such contexts there is no harm and may be much good. But such a community consensus is rapidly disappearing, and is often gone before local teachers or school officials actually acknowledge it.

The problems in our society, and more specifically in education, are massive and call for much more than a minute or two of prayer. Only the direct involvement of people of integrity and competence will quell the rising humanism in our public schools. There is, I believe, a real search for values in America today. As the *Reformed Journal* observed in July of 1981, "modern people who made the world safe for irreligion have found that religion has come back to haunt them."[1] The Christian's response must not be merely symbolic and superficial. A moment of formal, school-run prayer is hardly the solution or the approach needed.

From either a religious or political viewpoint, there is little to be gained by imposing such prayer times when significant minorities find them threatening. The gains are small compared with the alienation and divisiveness that may result. Much of the emotional opposition to school prayer may come from the middle-aged members of our society who remember how lonely they felt as the only Catholics in a Protestant schoolroom or the only Jews in a Christian environment.

There is no biblical directive that supports—and there is much common sense that rejects—utilizing the secular government to achieve a spiritual end. Those who believe that means and ends are intimately associated realize that the character of the fruit will reflect the root. Relying on secular educators to give meaning and vitality to school prayer might be akin to handing the Ark of the Covenant to Nebuchadnezzar for safekeeping. It is a mistake to hand the sacred and holy over to the careless, or, worse, to the profane.

Finally, Christians ought to be very cautious about the use of political power. Such means are not always improper; where the character of our community is clearly at issue, political power is perhaps a legitimate exercise of Christian responsibility. But where that power is used to force a devotional exercise on others, I wonder if evangelism and a Christian life-style would not be more vivid witnesses. When Christians do use political power, we should have goals that are related to a direct biblical command. There is no command to pray with schoolteachers.

WRONG FOCUS

School-supervised prayer is simply the wrong issue. It is frankly an idea whose time has come . . . and gone. Henry Steele Commanger, perhaps the most distinguished American historian, spoke at a conference on religious freedom held at the University of Southern California in 1981. Commanger challenged the religious groups represented, but chided them as well. "At a time when hunger, international terrorism and nuclear war threaten national survival, our best minds should not be called on to debate school prayer . . ."[2]

Many, including this author, are convinced that even if school prayers were truly spiritual—or at least harmless—the rush to reinstitute some sort of official school prayer time emerges from a dangerous misconception of the problem. Thus the popular sentiment for school prayer may be little more than a Band-aid on a more serious and intractable illness. But worse, it may create the illusion that some real gains have been made. Some are likely to feel the course has been changed, that we now are recovering our principled roots. This would be far from the truth. Scant evidence supports any fundamental change in the philosophical orientation of modern education or the instruction in schools of education, which create the basic policies and philosophies. While there are some encouraging signs of a return to basic education to assure reading and other skills, the general rush to humanistic process proceeds apace.

The banning of school prayers is in many ways a symbol, a highly visible mark of a change in the character of our whole society, not just in education. It is a change many like. But others find it disturbing, even frightening, as we rush headlong into a valueless, rootless future. I am saddened that the character of our society and our education is not conducive to a recognition of spiritual reality. I regret that acknowledging God's providence is no longer a national commitment.

The elimination of school prayers seems to signal that shift. But I do not believe it created the shift. Bill Bright of Campus Crusade is largely right in noting the dizzying downhill course of our society in the last two decades. I believe he is correct in saying that a misdirected education contributed something to that decline. But I believe the decline in school prayer is a consequence of a larger assault on moral and religious life in our nation, not the cause of it, as Bill Bright and many others suggest.

There is a dangerous tendency to look at surface manifestations and ignore the more basic trends and underlying movements in our culture. The abolition of school prayer had, in many schools, been accomplished by a combination of state court decisions, local choices, and apathy long before *Engel* v. *Vitale*. In some communities that retained such practices, the prayers may have been genuine expressions of faith, but in most places, real prayer, the real imploring of God to be present in education, had surely ceased before Chief Justice Earl Warren and Justice Hugo Black began tampering.

For years a growing secularism had been creeping into our society and education professionals were not immune to this disease. Many educators have rejected the Christian world view that "God is there, and he is not silent," to use Francis Schaeffer's terminology. This shifting of the higher education intelligentsia, and hence the schools, from theistic presuppositions to an alleged neutrality, but actual skepticism about theism, spelled the doom for any meaningful prayer in school.

There are other critical issues of religious liberty facing our society. There are serious threats to the rights of believers to practice their faith in the affairs of everyday life. My colleague, Samuel Ericsson, and I discussed these issues in *The Battle for Religious Liberty*. We pointed out that the courts have at times failed to see the dimensions of religious liberty in many issues. While zealously guarding free exercise claims, the courts and administrative officials have become enamored with the "separation of church and state," a phrase that has been the basis for penalties to religious practices in public life. But it is a woefully inadequate interpretation of the American experience to argue either that we have lost our religious liberty because of the school prayer decision or that the Supreme Court has somehow betrayed religion. The Court did not create the secularism in the universities of our nation that has sapped us of our moral vitality.

In fact, it is a mistake to view the law as the essential tool of our problems or solutions. Learned Hand, one of the most noted jurists in American history, declared, "I often wonder whether we do not rest our hopes too much upon constitutions, upon laws and upon courts. These are false hopes; believe me, these are false hopes."[3]

This is not to say that law does not shape our values. Indeed it does. The Supreme Court is an effective moral teacher: sometimes for good, as when it speaks of equality of races; sometimes for evil as when it allows the mass extermination of human life by barring almost all limits to abortion. The law is important as a guardian of values and a model of justice. But we ought to look deeper than statutes and court rulings to find the root causes of our problems.

Supporters of school prayer are certainly right in noting the crisis of our society and its need for an informing vision, which can give meaning to the concept of community and culture. They are right that only a spiritual reawakening can give that wholeness, that breadth of integrity and righteousness that exalts any people. They are correct that education without character is tragic.

But it is also quite evident that Christians must grasp prayer and its place in their lives in ways that far exceed a casual nod to God in school. Our prayer, our awareness of God, must be as Theophan the Recluse said, "with [us] as clearly as a toothache."

Perhaps in the despair and tragedy of our times, we should acknowledge the spiritual character of this struggle. Then we can release it into God's hands. Such recognition of the centrality of prayer for our nation, our schools, and our own lives must not be shunted off into little rituals. It surely must be earnest, persistent, imploring prayer. This is one action we can and must take.

What else ought we to do? Unfortunately, our task is broader and less focused than voting for an amendment. But it is not only broader, it's more lasting and fundamental. The full task cannot even be outlined, much less detailed here. Rather in the next chapters I would like to suggest areas of action that might achieve the goals many persons hope to accomplish.

13

The Real Voluntary
Prayer Issue

Let's begin this chapter with a multiple choice question. Which word should be written in the blank?

_____ in the public schools is "too dangerous to permit."
  a. drugs
  b. crime
  c. failing academic scores
  d. student prayer groups

If you answered drugs, crime, or failing academic scores, you forgot the Second Circuit Court of Appeals ruling in *Brandon* v. *Guilderland School District*. The court was not talking about school-organized prayers or state-written prayers. It was prohibiting students from gathering on their own initiative.

There is a very serious problem, a real threat to religious liberty in American schools today. But it does not focus on what the school can do; it focuses on the rights of students. The real issue is not what activities the school plans, but those it tries to stop. And, as I have noted, both courts and school administrators have prohibited students from exercising their right to meet at school during their free time to pray and/or study the Bible.

After all, it is one thing to say the school cannot write prayers or structure prayer times, but it is quite another to say that schools may—or must—impede students who wish to meet on their own time and pray. The courts have gone to ridiculous extremes to find "sponsorship" or "aid to religion" when the school is only allowing students to have the same rights to speak to God—or to each other about God—as students have to organize and talk about other subjects.

I have already mentioned two well-known cases (*Johnson* v. *Huntington Beach* and *Brandon* v. *Guilderland School District*) in which courts upheld school policies that discriminated against the rights of religious students. But there are many other cases where court decisions are having a devastating impact on the rights of young Christians to earnestly implore God for guidance and strength during these influential years of their lives. Unlike school-organized prayer cases, these are cases in which young people have made a deliberate choice to seek God's will in their lives and to pray for guidance.

In Williamsport, Pennsylvania, students applied for permission to start a student group called "Petros," which would meet before or after school or during a period designated for school club meetings. The school board refused.

In Anderson, South Carolina, a public high school has been threatened with a suit by the local Civil Liberties Union for opening its doors a half hour early each day for a student religious group's meeting.

At North Allegheny High School in Pittsburgh, a 1980-81 policy of permitting student groups, including a religious group, to meet before school was abandoned.

In Dixon, Illinois, the hometown of President Ronald Reagan, the local school board voted to ban all voluntary religious activities at schools.

All this is quite contrary to the constant declarations of many that "voluntary" prayer has not been banned. Only by reducing "voluntary" to "secret" are students allowed to pray. In fact, students have occasionally been advised that such activities, even when they are totally informal—such as on the lawn at lunch or at their locker or in their cars before going into school—are *unconstitutional!*

Is it really "dangerous" to allow a religious student group to seek fellowship together during the school day? Is it really "dangerous" to have such religious values be a part of the mix of student life? It would seem far more "dangerous" to exclude such values from the schools, as a dissenting Buddhist judge argued in the *Huntington Beach* case.

Isn't it far more dangerous to start supervising the content of speech? Or allowing students to organize and meet only when the speech has been properly purged of devotional references to God? (God's name may, of course, be used by students in less devotional ways. And certainly many athletic coaches paid by the state can cuss and swear with impunity. But by all means stop those dangerous students!) Isn't it infinitely more dangerous to seek to separate students from valuable moral resources? What is everyone so afraid of?

Brandon and *Huntington Beach* are effectively intimidating school boards across the country. Any time school boards consider these issues, an attorney is sure to mention these cases. When the Saddleback Valley, California, school district decided to adopt a policy permitting a variety of student groups to meet, including religious groups, the American Civil Liberties Union filed suit. A new school board changed the policy. For all its usual talk about civil liberties and students' rights, the ACLU is not much for liberty when a group of Christian students is involved. (The Washington Civil Liberties Union even opposed the rights of Christian students to meet at universities.)

The rights of students to genuine voluntary prayer must be established, unless we are to insist that students be as neutral, as secular, perhaps as confused, as the schools. Some have wondered why students cannot simply pray at home. Isn't that enough? opponents ask. The questions of *why* they wish to pray at school and *whether* they couldn't do it elsewhere are largely irrelevant to their constitutional rights. You cannot deny my right to speak at a particular place merely by saying that you will let me speak elsewhere.

But beyond that, students spend a substantial part of their waking hours at school and in transit to and from the school. Combined with after-school athletic and club activities, school may easily demand nearly all of a typical student's day. Many schools have "closed campuses," and will not allow students to leave the school property during free periods. To deprive students of the opportunity to seek mutual religious encouragement during this time is to deny them this sustenance during most of their available time. Besides, the school atmosphere is precisely the kind of setting in which they need fellowship and prayer support. Would anyone oppose a student group that sought to meet at school to resist the use of drugs? Would anyone tell them to do it at home? Hardly! They would recognize that such meetings were helpful in developing values and opposing debilitating pressures.

As of this writing, the court decisions seem to indicate that religious speech is not entitled to the same protection in our schools that political speech is. This is most surprising, since student rights have been dramatically defended by other court decisions, especially by a 1969 case, *Tinker* v. *Des Moines*. In that case, the Supreme Court struck down attempts by the school board to bar students from wearing black armbands in opposition to the Vietnam War. The Court declared that students do not leave their constitutional rights at the door of the school. The school could not deny students their rights of speech unless the school could show that the exercise substantially disrupted the school's operation or significantly interfered with the rights of other students. *Tinker* was a declaration of student rights of free speech, however unpopular. Yet when students wish to pray, they are barred.

These California and New York decisions and similar school policies must continue to be challenged until a court, most properly the United States Supreme Court, will recognize the tragedy of these penalties and grant religious students the same rights as other students.

LUBBOCK, TEXAS, MAY PROVIDE AN ANSWER

It is important to recognize that these cases have involved school administrations that had chosen, for whatever reasons, to prohibit students from meeting for religious purposes. But what if a school wishes to be evenhanded and *grant* all student groups the same rights and limitations? That was the desire of the Lubbock Independent School District. In 1980 it adopted a policy that stated:

> The school board permits students to gather at the school with supervision either before or after regular hours on the same basis as other groups as determined by the school administration to meet for any educational, moral, religious or ethical purpose so long as attendance at such meetings is voluntary.

But this equal rights policy was challenged by the usual friends of liberty, the Civil Liberties Union. The Lubbock Civil Liberties Union sued. As I noted earlier, a United States district court upheld the policy as neutral and a permissible accommodation. But the United States Court of Appeals reversed and held that the policy was impermissible. The court of appeals said that the purpose of this provision was to promote religious meetings, and, therefore, it advanced religion since the meetings would carry the "implicit approval" of school officials. The court even noted its concern that students might be intimidated and lose their freedom of choice if they saw the football captain or a drama-club actress participating. It was a "captive audience," the court said. To hear the court talk, the school sounds like a prison or a factory of automatons.

Thus, the court of appeals went one step further than *Brandon*, and declared that a school district may not only restrict the rights of religious students to meet before or after school, it *must*. So much for student rights of equal protection and free speech! The decision flies in the face of almost all other free speech cases, where courts have struck down any restrictions (prior restraint) on free speech based on the *content* of that speech. Yet here it is solely the religious content that bars students from meeting.

The decision also furthers the myth that high school students are totally unable to distinguish programs sponsored by the school from those that the school merely allows to occur. We need to remind the courts that we are talking about high school students who are nearly old enough to vote, old enough, the courts have said, to decide for themselves whether to get an abortion—but not old enough to choose freely whether to participate in a before-school prayer group!

Regardless of what the court says, there is no implication in the *Lubbock* case that the school approves of the particular religious faith of the students any more than it endorses the political views of the Republican Club or the values of the Student Athletic Association or the French Club. Although it is hard to imagine that a group of elementary students could organize a club without school control, no one in recent years has accused high school students of being overly intimidated by administrators or teachers.

The court's conclusion that the mere location of the group

meetings at a school creates an atmosphere of endorsement is overly simplistic, unless the school is prepared to be charged with endorsing every opinion and act of a student group on school property. Neither does the fact that students must attend school mean that they must attend the meetings of every club at the school. Many groups, like the athletic teams, cheerleaders, and drama clubs, are selective and not open to every student. Nor have courts held schools responsible for the opinions of a student political club when it endorses a controversial candidate for some office.

The *Lubbock* decision is now in the process of appeal, and will go to the United States Supreme Court for a final determination. The *Tinker* case said a student doesn't leave his *constitutional rights* at the door of the school. *Lubbock* will decide whether or not he leaves his *faith* at the door of the school.

We need an opinion at the high school level that is as clear and decisive as *Widmar* v. *Vincent*, the case in which the Supreme Court sustained the rights of Christian student groups to meet at the University of Missouri. The university had refused to recognize a Christian group, Cornerstone, as a student organization, alleging that their use of school facilities and status as a student club would constitute an impermissible level of support by the government and, therefore, violate the Establishment Clause of the Constitution. The Supreme Court (in an 8-1 decision) struck down that argument, and declared that when the university allows students to meet and organize on campus, it cannot discriminate against religious students. Worship (speech to God) is a protected free speech liberty. The same principles are at issue in the high school cases.

It seems critical that every legal effort be made to point out to the Supreme Court that the mere fact that students happen to be at the school while speaking to God does not constitute some real or apparent endorsement by the state of what those students say. The Court should realize that the state may not discriminate against such religious students, for to do so denies them their rights of free speech and equal protection of the law. Such hostility would seem to violate the Establishment Clause of the First Amendment, since the Supreme Court has held the clause prohibits government from either "aiding" or "inhibiting" religion.

An example of a legally defensible policy that might be

adopted by a school board to allow religious students to meet on high school premises is included at the end of this chapter. Parents might suggest such a policy to their local board.

LEGISLATIVE ACTION

In addition to decisions in critical cases like *Lubbock*, another approach involves federal legislation, which would seek to apply the principles of equal protection and free speech rights set forth for university students in *Widmar* v. *Vincent* to the high school setting.

While such a bill could be overturned by a court, it is within the power of Congress to engage in fact-finding and policy-making where federal funds are involved. A bill asserting that high school students have sufficient maturity to fall within a Widmar-type policy might shape court evaluations, and would serve as an encouragement to those school boards who wish to be evenhanded but have been intimidated by actual or threatened lawsuits.

Possible legislation has been drafted by various bodies. One example states:

> No public secondary school receiving federal financial assistance, which generally allows groups of students to meet during non-instructional periods, shall discriminate against any meeting of students on the basis of the content of speech at the meeting, provided that the meeting shall be voluntary and orderly and that no activity which is in and of itself unlawful need be permitted.

The proposal limits the effect to schools that receive federal financial assistance; therefore, it would not attempt to govern all schools. The proposal also limits applicability to schools that "generally" allow student meetings, because the Supreme Court's decision in *Widmar* focused on the fact that the university had generally allowed student groups to meet and was now discriminating against a religious student group, simply on the basis of content of speech. Thus, if a school wished, it might adopt a policy that did not generally allow student meetings. Then they would not be compelled to permit religious student groups. The statute further limits itself to students functioning in groups, and does not focus on the involvement of teachers or of the right of students to speak outside of a group context.

The statute is not a blank check. It does not require a school to allow student meetings that disrupt the educational purposes of the school or substantially interfere with the rights of others. If some of the worst fears of opponents of such religious groups materialized—harassment of students or religious divisions that substantially and directly impeded the school's academic program—then the school could limit the student activities.

Christians should watch for such bills and encourage their senators and representatives to support them. Writing letters or signing petitions can make a difference, and such actions are the Christian citizen's privilege—and duty.

This does not seem to be a time in our history when we can afford to actively resist students' desires to seek spiritual strength among their fellow students. Official school spirituality we can do without. But we must not handcuff a student's spirit! Let's battle those posing as civil libertarians who seek to stop students from praying.

MODEL POLICY ON STUDENT USE OF
SECONDARY SCHOOL FACILITIES
FOR RELIGIOUS PURPOSES

The following section is a sample wording of a school board policy on the use of secondary school facilities for religious purposes. Parents could submit this sample if the local school board is considering establishing a clear policy or altering an existing one. This sample policy could, of course, be altered to fit the specific situation.

The first item in the preamble points out the situation in which such a policy formation or change is most likely to occur: a case in which students request to meet or in which students already meet and their right to do so is challenged.

The purpose of the preamble is to give rational, secular reasons for the board's policy and to show that the board is not attempting to establish or aid religion.

The policy itself outlines the legitimate, constitutional roles of both the school and the religious students' club in specific areas.

PREAMBLE: The Policy regarding student use of school facilities has been developed in response to the concerns of students, parents, and members of the community.

The Board Policy is based upon the following facts:

1. Secondary school students have requested to meet on their school premises for religious purposes.

2. The United States Supreme Court has ruled that students possess their basic constitutional rights while at school and may exercise those rights if they do not materially or substantially interfere with the requirements of appropriate discipline in the operation of the school and with the rights of others. In addition to the applicable constitutional rights of free speech and assembly, this policy recognizes the constitutional provision against the establishment of religion and the provision for the free exercise of religion.

3. The students would meet without sponsorship by their schools and without any endorsement or any participation by

school authorities other than normally involved when students are present on school property. There is no indication that students at the school would think that these meetings are endorsed by or in any way represent the school.

4. The students' meetings would create no cost to the schools. There is no additional wear or tear or operational expense, since the students will be on campus someplace else if not in the meeting place. No special supervision is required nor any services supplied. The students would not have any sort of school financial account.

5. These students have shared moral values and beliefs that differ significantly from the values of many, perhaps the majority, of their classmates. Yet they are compelled by law to attend school and to associate daily with students whose beliefs and behavior contradict theirs. Psychological studies and common experience confirm the effects of peer pressure upon students whose values are different from the student culture, particularly during adolescence.

6. The predominant function of these student groups is to permit the students to identify with other students who have spiritual, moral, religious, ethical, and other values similar to theirs. This will create a peer identity within the school culture (which may otherwise be cool, if not hostile, to their beliefs and attitudes) and give these students the support they need to survive and mature in the educational context within which they find themselves.

In reaching the Policy below, the Board has further concluded (a) that the student meetings in question will have no measurable impact on nonparticipating students, (b) that it is not the proper role for the school to monitor or unnecessarily restrict student expression that does not interfere with the educational process, (c) that part of the educational process in a pluralistic society means that students need to be exposed to and associate with students of other moral and religious beliefs, just as they do with students of other racial and political backgrounds, but without being subject to coercion to change their beliefs involuntarily, and (d) that all students should be treated equally in their private conduct.

SCHOOL BOARD POLICY

Use of secondary school facilities by students who meet for religious purposes shall be permitted in accordance with the following principles and guidelines:

1. No school shall discriminate against any student on the basis of race, color, creed, religion, sex, or national origin in the assignment or use of school facilities.

2. No school shall deny any student in the use of school facilities, the constitutional guarantees of freedom of religion, speech, press, association, petition, and equal protection of the laws or restrict these freedoms in any manner except as essential in the performance of the school's educational purposes, to avoid substantial interference with the necessary school discipline.

3. All students, whether as school sponsored clubs, nonsponsored student groups, or individuals, shall have equal access to school facilities under neutral regulations to be adopted by each school regarding the time, place, and manner of use, for proper allocation of available space and supervision.

4. No school shall sponsor or officially endorse any religious practice or activity by any student nor sponsor or officially recognize any student group that meets for religious purpose. Lack of official sponsorship, endorsement, or recognition shall not be used to deny any student or nonsponsored student group equal access to school facilities.

5. No school shall compel or encourage any student to participate in any religious activity. No student or employee shall intentionally deceive or coerce a student to attend a religious meeting or to adopt a particular religious belief or ideology.

6. Student use of school facilities shall not be regulated on the

basis of the content of the students' meetings, except that the school may terminate meetings that are immoral, violent (or advocate violence), or interfere with the educational process. Religious speech shall receive the same rights and protections as political and all other speech, including private voluntary prayer, reading from religious or political books, and speaking about political or religious topics. The school may prohibit outside speakers at student meetings if the school finds that the appearance of the speaker will incite violence or interfere with the educational process.

7. School employees, while acting in their official capacities and performing their duties as school employees, shall not sponsor, support, or participate in religious practices or activities involving students.

8. Student use of school facilities for religious purposes shall be supervised, as necessary, by the school to maintain order on the school premises. Meetings may be supervised in the same manner as the school supervises student behavior generally, as in hallways, lounges, study rooms, libraries, lunchrooms, or open areas on the campus. Nonsponsored student groups shall secure and maintain an adult supervisor acceptable to the school.

9. The school may publish the times and locations of the meetings of any school sponsored clubs, nonsponsored student groups, or other students who have been assigned use of school facilities. The school shall not otherwise announce or report the activities of any nonsponsored student groups in *official school publications*. All student activities, including nonsponsored activities, may be announced or reported in *any student publications* or through the use of any permitted means of student communication, such as bulletin boards, posters, flyers, and oral announcements.

10. The school may prohibit or regulate in any manner the collection or expenditure of money by or on behalf of any student, nonsponsored student groups, or school sponsored club relating to any activity that takes place in school facilities or on school premises.

11. Any student or nonsponsored student group using school facilities shall reimburse the school for any additional costs incurred by the school because of such use. No school funds shall be expended by or on behalf of nonsponsored student groups.

14

A Christian Commitment
To Education

Education is indeed powerful. It can build or belittle, nurture or destroy. The American commitment to education, however exaggerated at times, is something of which we may be justly proud. Public schools have been a part of our country since 1647 when the Massachusetts General Court adopted an act that established a system of common education.

But this noble heritage ought not to render education immune to criticism, and indeed there is much to complain about. "Let us now bury the public schools," insists educator Howard Means. They are staffed by the disillusioned, weighed down by a bloated bureaucracy, are committed to nothing, and producing "numskulls." It is a "swamp hole," he declares.[1]

But as common as such complaints are, public education is not going to be buried—at least in the foreseeable future.

Regardless of the touted explosion of private education, public schools are almost certainly going to continue to play a major—probably *the* major—role in the education of America's children. Frank Gaebelein, a leader in Christian education, noted that "evangelical Christian education is only a minority of a minority, a little drop in a big bucket."[2]

We neglect the public schools at the peril of our communities. If we care about our national life, about our youth, then we must care about public education. It is our civic as well as our spiritual duty. Christians simply must begin to recognize the responsibility and opportunity for Christian involvement in public education.

149

INVESTING IN EDUCATION

"We should keep in mind the word *public* in public education. It means *the schools belong to us*," George van Alstine reminds us. And if anything is needed in education, it is people who will commit themselves to making an impact—people who will give of their energies for the long haul, building competence and relationships, and "paying their dues."

We do not need more adventurers and explorers; we need settlers who see the tremendous needs in public education, persons who are ready for a long-term commitment to affecting this vital aspect of our culture. We have not relinquished our rights to shape that educational process, so we should not be timid or apologetic about involvement. We have the only credential needed: citizenship. And many of us have an added credential: we are parents. In 1925 the Supreme Court upheld the right of parents to control the education of their children (*Pierce* v. *Society of Sisters*).

The Court said: "Liberty . . . excludes any general power of the state to standardize its children. . . . [T]he child is not the mere creature of the state; those who nurture him . . . have the right . . . to recognize and prepare him for additional obligations."

Those committed to education will often be parents and neighbors, just "plain folk" who make their wishes known at Parent Teacher Association meetings or school board hearings. One school board member told your author recently that his board had a clear strategy for dealing with parental agitation. An open meeting would be held, at which many vocal parents could express their complaints. But the board would postpone action. A second meeting would find the number of complaining parents greatly reduced, and by the third meeting the interest would be gone! The issues are simply too complex and the political realities too immense to expect that any real contribution or change will be made unless the parents and other interested parties make a sustained commitment.

Such a commitment could very well make a difference. When *Publishers Weekly* surveyed 1,900 public school administrators and librarians in 1981, 22 percent of the respondents reported challenges to books or other classroom materials. And 33 percent of this number indicated that these challenges had resulted in changes in books and materials! The survey noted that most of the challenges were by individual parents. One person can make himself or herself heard, it seems.

Unfortunately, parental involvement all too often means parents are expected to do as they are told: prepare a dish for a potluck and attend a couple of PTA meetings a year.[3] Instead parents need to understand what is happening in their schools and to note the educational content and processes that are being developed. Parental involvement is work, but it is an investment in our children and our communities.

ACTING RESPONSIBLY

It's a "cold war . . . parents versus teachers," complained a guidance counselor, describing the current climate in schools to Ethel Herr.[4] Parental involvement today may be viewed with suspicion. Certainly the style of parental comment may at times have placed educators in a defensive mood, and some of the attacks on education have been irresponsible and uninformed. John Fentriss Gardner noted the irony of school resistance to parent involvement: "It is a paradox that those who are the most fanatical about the necessity for the democratic school system are also most distrustful of the people."[5] Hopefully, a responsible involvement will not be viewed as instituting a cold war.

A greater degree of personal kindness and a greater degree of intellectual ferocity is the need of modern man, declared G. K. Chesterton.[6] His counsel should be well heard for those who wish to influence education. I take it to be similar to the biblical admonition to be wise as serpents and harmless as doves. Unfortunately, too many educational critics have lacked the quality of kindness, and their ferocity has been less than intellectual. Those who cursed the Engels (plaintiffs in the first school prayer case to reach the Supreme Court) and wished polio upon their children, did not witness well to the love of God!

Kindness ought to mean avoiding impugning motives or attacking the character of opponents. It ought to mean being gracious in both victory and defeat. It ought to mean a genuine concern for those with whom we are in intellectual struggle. Unfortunately, tactics used in other political and social struggles have utilized intimidation and power plays, which are hardly becoming to those whose goal is growth in the fruits of the Spirit. Christians must constantly examine both their goals and their means.

Chesterton's second phrase, *intellectual ferocity*, connotes both the intensity of the struggle and a level of insight that reaches beyond personalities to great issues. At first there seems to be a tension between intellectual ferocity and kindness. Too often we think of kindness as abdication and silence. But the struggles of our day call for engagement, not acquiescence. We need to learn how to become dissenters—and ferocious ones at that.

Dissent is a rich American tradition. Our very democratic processes require it. Our Constitution protects it. Citizenship demands it. Dissent may seem impolite: it stirs up trouble; it irritates people. But without dissent our character as a society is in jeopardy.

Dissent is also a biblical tradition. The prophets were not noted for their "me-too-ism," but for their capacity to say no to their culture. They loved their nation. They were committed to its welfare. But that commitment required that they speak powerfully and directly. As children we sang of such dissent: "Dare to be a Daniel; Dare to stand alone."

As Christians, we must begin to cultivate the capacity for creative and kindly dissent. However we must beware that a dissident stance does not wipe out kindness and infect our personalities with an inordinate stridentness, a defensive labeling of all opponents, and a persecution complex. It is not easy to be a dissident and still be winsome. Dissidents often become myopic: unable to see any merit in an opponent, defensive about any criticism, suspicious of others, and unwilling to compromise when necessary. Often, they become downright obnoxious!

"If you can't stand the heat, then get out of the kitchen," was President Harry Truman's favorite admonition to faint-hearted cabinet members and congressmen. Surely no person can seek to provide leadership in any controversial area without experiencing conflict and attack. For those who become involved in the educational arena, there's plenty of heat in the kitchen. You'd better prepare for verbal exchanges: for being classed with the ignorant, the unclean, the simplistic—and worst of all, the "unprogressive." You'd better be ready to stand—and still to love.

Be ready, because the complaints from conservative and parent groups about the predominance of behavioralist aspects in education have begun to stir up the troops on the other side.

And, believe me, they are as determined and angry as their opponents. Katharine Hepburn in a July 1982 direct mail letter called for a "public impact program" as part of a "massive educational effort" to attack the philosophies of Moral Majority style groups who are attacking "one of our most fundamental individual rights" through their support of the human life effort. With amazing naivete Hepburn says, "most reasonable people would agree" that the notion that abortion is a sin is a "simple outdated platitude."

As I mentioned in chapter three, Sidney Simon likewise collected all his stamps and mailed a fundraising letter to finance the formation of the National Coalition for Democracy in Education. The organization's brochure is as American as apple pie: a sun with a smiling face and an American flag waving in the breeze over a happy schoolhouse. The purpose is likewise gentle and kind: to advocate democracy, freedom, and good education. But read a little further. The affiliated organizations, not surprisingly, are the Association for Humanistic Education, Association for Humanistic Education and Development, Association for Humanistic Psychology, Effectiveness Training, Inc., and others.

THINKING FOUNDATIONALLY

Intellectual ferocity, however, does not mean merely growling. It means a real grappling with what are actually quite difficult issues. It means political give-and-take. There are too many in the Christian community who offer simplistic analyses of and answers to truly urgent questions. Such persons play into the hands of opponents. For example, in the area of textbook and library book criticism, some well-meaning parents have objected to such classics as *Huckleberry Finn* and the writings of Aleksandr Solzhenitsyn. These extremists are widely quoted to show the alleged irrationality of "far right fundamentalists."

What are the central issues and questions? They are so basic, they are largely ignored. What is education? What is the role of the state and the family in education? Is there any ascertainable truth? And if so, how do we find it?

Not until we explore education as a nation and as a Christian community can we hope to examine the relationship of education to moral values and inevitably to religion. We won't know what a good textbook is, or what the curriculum ought to be, or whether Johnny is really learning, until we have answers to these questions.

C.S. Lewis observed that, at present, our society continues to clamor for the very qualities it renders impossible. With "a sort of ghastly simplicity we remove the organ and demand the function . . . we castrate and bid the geldings be fruitful."[7]

We seek a just society, but we eliminate religion and morals from our educational system. We seek brotherhood, but we eliminate all teaching that each individual is a child of God, fearfully and wonderfully created.

If these eternal truths are gone, then all is relative. All is process. All is personal choice. *All is self.* The result may be what Bruno Bettelheim, the noted psychiatrist-educator, observed in the literature of the schools: "There is no good or evil. . . . Everyone's lukewarm. . . . From the books you'd never know there's so much evil in this society."[8]

Values seem to have been shunted off to the home or the church. Of course values belong there, but they belong as well to the world of education. As long ago as 1938 commentator Wolfgang Kohler spoke of a "crisis of scholarship" in which the scholars have left the questions of value and meaning, of morality and metaphysics and retired into their own little world.[9]

Thus before we rush to the school board or create our list of "least desirable books," we must work on these questions as a Christian community so we can contribute our insights to the educational world. We need to create a vision of education that emerges out of our convictions about the nature of man and the character of education.

We must form these convictions through study and thought —through the reading of books about education and the discussion of ideas with other Christians. A church forum on public education's goals and methods, perhaps led by a teacher or other church member familiar with the educational field, could contribute much to Christians' ability to speak up intelligently about local school policies.

Christians can keep alert to current issues in education through newsletters such as *Education Today,* published by The Heritage Foundation (513 C St., N.E., Washington, D.C. 20002) under the direction of educational consultant Onalee McGraw, and *Vision,* a publication of the Christian Educators Association (P.O. Box 2226, Newport Beach, CA 92663).

A response that has integrity must also cease the blanket condemnation of public education. Much is good, even excellent, in education today. Let us proudly acknowledge real advances in education: programs to meet the special needs of the gifted, the handicapped, and the mentally retarded; creative and imaginative teaching methods that make the work of learning fun. I can think of teachers in my life whose efforts went largely unrewarded and who have rarely been thanked for putting up with me and my kids.

A responsible approach needs to avoid as well the charges of conspiracy, which are frequently utilized. No doubt there are those who have specific agendas for the use of schools to promote their ideologies, but few teachers and administrators are conscious co-conspirators. Most of these people want to be effective; they want to see education improved. They may at times be defensive and concerned about their job security and advancement. They may have absorbed the secularist biases of higher education. But many are simply overwhelmed by the demands from all sides that come upon them. They need support from the Christian community, not just accusation.

ADVOCATES OF LIBERTY

"A vast religio-political conspiracy to deny pluralism" is what Christian author Virginia Mollenkott called the rise of the Moral Majority and its intellectual cousins. The charge is not entirely fair. Who are the real opponents of pluralism in education? Which ideas have been withdrawn from public education? The ideas of moral relativism or the concepts of traditional morality? The misapplication of the principle of separation of church and state and an educational leadership that is unsympathetic to traditional values and morals have virtually eliminated religion and morals from the classroom.

The moral perspectives the right is advocating were not only shared by the prevailing culture but enforced by law until recent years. For example, when conservatives resist pornography, abortion, or sexually explicit language in schoolbooks, they are hardly to be characterized as "censors"—unless one wishes to include most of the decisions of United States courts until the last couple of decades.

It is the conservative who has sought to maintain the cultural perspective that shaped the moral character of our nation. One may ask if they are right or wrong or if new times require new public policies or if their tactics are fair, but let's dispense with simplistic charges of narrow censorship.

On the other hand, I believe pluralism is here to stay in American life. Efforts to create a public educational model that ignores this reality are doomed to failure. Instead, Christians ought to acknowledge and even defend this pluralism. We ought to insist that Christian perspectives have an equal opportunity to share in this marketplace of ideas. As University of Virginia Professor David Little observed, "this state of affairs [the exclusion of religious ideas from education] . . . hardly seems fair. Why should those who nurture students and direct their destinies with reference to nonreligious beliefs be favored over those who espouse religious beliefs? In terms of simple justice, why should [utilitarian philosopher Jeremy] Bentham's views be publically supported in preference to Roman Catholic or Lutheran or Mennonite views, just because Bentham's views happen not, in one plausible sense, to be religious? And if such bald discrimination in favor of non-religious principles is the implication of the Establishment Clause, then perhaps that clause needs some serious rethinking."[10]

David Little has properly identified the central problem. The exclusion of *formal* religion from public education, which in my opinion is just, has led to the improper exclusion of ideas and values that derive from religious convictions. That has left the field, almost by definition, to ideas that are nonreligious, or even counterreligious. Is that pluralism? Surely ideas central to our cultural history should not be penalized because they are also a part of religious beliefs. Neither should ideas be excluded simply because people have committed their lives to them. In the area of sex education, for example, should sound educational policy or constitutional law require the elimination of views that see sexual relationships outside of marriage as wrong and destructive to human character and the family?

Let us become those who are truly liberal, truly open, to exposing students to multiple points of view in school. Let the opposition be the limiters and constrainers. It is ironic that the supposed liberals who tout the schools as a marketplace of ideas and advocate the need for students to explore all kinds of options exclude, for example, the creationist perspective from classroom discussion. The pamphlet of the National Coalition for

Democracy in Education advocates a student's right to "be exposed to a variety of viewpoints in contemporary issues," but resists state efforts to provide pluralism in views of origins.

A far better approach to the problem of school literature and textbooks is to advocate pluralism and encourage the inclusion of literature in libraries and courses that develops alternative, even religious, views. School authorities, librarians, and curriculum writers may well resist such genuine pluralism. But the Supreme Court has clearly acknowledged the constitutionality of the study of religious ideas and their impact on society. There is no bar to an objective examination of religious perspectives. There is only a reluctance on the part of educators—and perhaps a lack of adequate materials. Let us stop trying to silence the views of the secularists and try instead to assure that alternatives are presented. We need not fear the debate. We have nothing to hide.

A commitment to pluralism means that we cannot expect the schools to exclusively adopt our perspectives on all issues, or totally avoid views with which we disagree. Tolerance is a requirement of a pluralistic culture. If we want our views to have a chance, we must allow others that opportunity as well.

With these general approaches to the educational system—responsible action and foundational and pluralistic thinking—parents have been able to influence public education. The specifics of such encounters are many, but a few will be enumerated in the next chapter, which predicts a new phenomenon in American society: the parent revolution.

15

The Parent Revolution

We've had an industrial revolution, an American revolution, and now Jeane Westin predicts the coming parent revolution in her book of that title. More than anything else, parents need to regain control of their own children and their own homes and family lives.

Parents have been increasingly insecure about their roles, afraid to discipline, and intimidated by the "experts," Westin says. "For the last 25 years, the . . . traditional family has been seen as the corrupter of children's lives."

Examples of this misconception are reflected in court rulings and the attitudes of child development and educational specialists. Judge Lisa Richette of Pennsylvania's First Judicial District ruled: "If there is a least detrimental alternative, remove the child and don't worry about the rights of parents. The child belongs to society. The parents were only biological producers."[1] Then there's Edward Zigler, former director of the United States Office of Child Development, who openly declared, "Children do not belong to parents."

In California a 1979 law allows children of the ages of fourteen to eighteen to "divorce" their parents, and a Washington State Court gave a child the same opportunity. Sweden has gone even further, outlawing spanking and prohibiting parents from exposing their children to "humiliating treatment," which apparently includes sending a child to bed without dinner. The "kiddie-lib" movement has been increasingly active since Richard Farson published his seminal statement, *Birthrights,* in 1974. Farson's list of children's rights includes sexual freedom,

freedom from education, and the right to alternative home environments.

The idea of family licensing has even been suggested to protect children from unfit parents. Jerry Berghman of Bowling Green University has suggested some minimum requirements: an IQ above 80, a salary of at least $8,000 a year, no serious emotional problems, and an understanding of how to care for a baby.

Jeane Westin strongly urges parents to disregard the advice of such "so-called" experts. Parent power isn't responsible for the corruption of children. In fact, she believes that the "shoe belongs on the opposite foot. . . . Our intimidation by the youth culture and its promoters—the forces of expert advice givers, government, schools and the media—is what has corrupted our families and brought us to the brink of parent revolution."[2] Westin says the parent revolution must become the "counter culture of the 1980's." It's either that or the "new family dark age."[3] We must firmly and decisively reject "our youth oriented society," which "collaborates to bankrupt traditional family values" with its narcissism and frantic consumption of pleasure without meaning.

Westin accuses the law and religion of failing to support the family and parents. The church, she says, "is so anxious to attract and hold an audience that it sits on its traditional standards. . . . The support once given parents by organized religion was supplanted by human-potential therapies, which assumed the trappings of religion—rebirth, spiritual growth, salvation, and the power of love—without adding the essential ingredient of belief in something or someone beyond self." Religion, thus psychologized, has lost its power to support parents. It's simply a religion of personal development. Thus the need for the 1980s is for parents to "recreate a family ethos that will act as a fortress against outside disruptive forces."[4]

Where are the families who have created a Christian ethos to protect children against the disruptive forces in our society? Where are families who search the Scriptures together and open their lives to the Spirit?

Christian parents need to remember the biblical admonition to teach children the faith in Deuteronomy 6:6-9.

And these words which I command you this day

shall be upon your heart; and you shall teach
them diligently to your children, and shall talk
of them when you sit in your house, and when
you walk by the way, and when you lie down,
and when you rise. And you shall bind them as
a sign upon your hand, and they shall be as
frontlets between your eyes. And you shall
write them on the doorposts of your house and
on your gates (RSV).

The teaching of the Spirit is not simply a time set aside; it is
a life set aside. Our children will grow spiritually if the Word of
God is written on the posts of our homes and is always before us
as frontlets. This teaching in Deuteronomy was given at a time
when the state structure was supportive of and informed by the
faith of Israel. How much more essential it is now that the
media, the educational structure, and the whole ethos of our
society is so often apathetic, if not hostile, to the life of the
Spirit.

Parents need to recommit themselves to greater participation in the emotional, intellectual, and spiritual growth of their
children.

I am talking about more than the simplistic suggestion,
"Have you hugged your child today?" although that's an excellent beginning and a critical component. I am talking about
helping children to understand what is happening around them
and developing gifts of discernment and insight and wisdom.

I am frankly more concerned about helping a child evaluate
and judge than preserving the child from offensive values in
literature. A child who knows raw secularism and narcissism
when it emerges is better prepared for life and witness than the
child who has been insulated from it.

BUILDING A SUBCULTURE

We must also recognize that a subculture like the Christian
faith needs its informing traditions, rituals, and celebrations. It
needs its rules and customs and habits, which identify the community and appropriately label it. We have lost our special
celebrations and holidays—Christmas and Easter—largely to
commercialism, and tragically some of us have belittled the importance of such symbols.

A look at the Old or New Testaments will quickly show the importance attached to occasions of memory and worship, of symbols and rituals. Of course, they can become empty, but they also remind us of our history and our faith. Like Israel, we need to have our history marked with stones (such as the Ebenezer raised by Joshua to remind the Israelites of the victory God gave them over the Philistines), which elicit questions from our society and our children about our relationship with God and his great acts on our behalf.

All of this is built on an assumption that is not sufficiently recognized: the Christian community has become a minority people. We are used to thinking of ourselves as the mainstream, the majority, the great middle. But in fact, we are a peculiar people, strangers and aliens. Our identity is no more of this American world than it was of a Roman world or a Russian world. We are grasping at illusions if we believe that the state, through the public school or any other institution, will reflect the uniqueness of our commitments and help us do our task. They will not help, and if they tried, they would botch it. Instead we must learn to thrive as a minority people: to gain our strength and character not because we dominate our culture, but rather because we have the Spirit within us and among us. We must learn what every Jew has always known and what every first century Christian and believer in the Soviet Union or China learned: how to nurture a lively and joyful faith in the midst of alien principalities and powers.

APPEALING TO CAESAR

Parents have the right to effect change in education as well as in the home. We can "appeal to Caesar" to change school policy as Paul did when his rights as a Roman citizen were denied in Caesarea. If parents' rights or the rights of their children are being violated, Christians have the same right to appeal to the courts that atheists have.

In fact, courts have repeatedly been forced to deal with complex issues of religion, parental rights, and education. In a landmark case, *West Virginia* v. *Barnette*, Justice Robert Jackson noted: "As government pressure toward unity becomes greater, so strife becomes more bitter as to whose unity it shall be."

The case raised a significant question of religious liberty:

whether or not the school could compel a student, Barnette, to participate in the Pledge of Allegiance against religious convictions. The Supreme Court said no; the state could not compel a person to make a statement contrary to that person's religious belief. The issues raised in *Barnette* again become urgent now that students may be required to engage in activities the state sees as religiously neutral even though the student and his or her parents find the actions objectionable.

The student's right to be excused from such activities is hotly debated. In March of 1982, for example, the Iowa House Education Committee rejected a proposal to allow a student to be excused from any course that "conflicts with the pupil's religious beliefs." The proposal's sponsor, Representative Karen Mann, indicated the expanded rights were important to protect religious minorities. But critics, like Representative Robert Anderson, said it would "allow your religion to decide whether you come into contact with other people, other ideas."

As school policies in some communities become increasingly offensive to some religious groups, our rights of religious liberty become more critical. Few persons are aware of these rights or how they may be effectively exercised (see *Battle for Religious Liberty* for a more complete analysis of our religious rights). Fortunately, the courts have generally been diligent in protecting student rights in public education.

The impact of law on education extends far beyond direct questions of religion and education and the Religion Clauses of the First Amendment. Court decisions and statutes have established other important rights: the protection of the privacy of students' educational records and the parents' rights to see these records, parental rights to review certain educational materials prepared by federal agencies, limits on the kinds of psychological testing that may be done with students, and the rights of students to a hearing and due process of law when they have been accused of major offenses. Some state legislatures or boards of education have established other rights: a parent's right to teach children at home, a student's right to be excused from religiously objectionable school activities, and a limit to the extent of permissible discipline.

State legislatures, school boards, and state educational bodies also create extensive regulations that affect education, so parents ought to become informed and involved in shaping these policies. Participation in school board policymaking can be a vital contribution to effective community-oriented education. Onalee McGraw in her monograph, "Secular Humanism and the Schools," described what one community in Frederick County, Maryland, did to develop guidelines for curricular development. Using a low-key approach, citizens began to express their concerns to board members, urging a comprehensive policy to protect parents' and students' rights in the face of what they felt were illegitimate uses of experimental psychological techniques in education. The policies and guidelines finally adopted were:

1. Persuasive techniques based on the religion of humanism are not legitimate areas of curriculum in the Frederick County School System.

   Secular humanism is defined as a religion that denies the existence of God and bestows that role to the individual.

   Any persuasion of humanism that promotes a religious or irreligious belief is in violation of the constitutional separation of church and state.

2. Valuing, values clarification, and moral education will not be taught in the Frederick County School System as courses in and of themselves or through a series of contrived situations without specific approval by the Board of Education.

   Contrived techniques should not be used for the indoctrination of values or to bring about social change or to explore social structures and inner conflicts, which constitute an invasion of privacy. Valuing, as it naturally emerges in valid instructional settings, will be considered an appropriate and useful teaching strategy.

3. Situation ethics, in a precisely defined religious sense, is not appropriate to public-school use and is strictly prohibited.

   The consideration of situations and circumstances that arise in curricular areas that cause students to engage in problem-solving activities and make resultant decisions (some of which have moral and social implications) must be handled wisely and judiciously. Issues that invade one's privacy or cause emotional trauma must be avoided.

4. Group counseling, when conducted by carefully selected and trained personnel and strictly monitored by qualified consultants, will be offered to certain students who have obtained written parental consent. Every caution should be exercised so that this program does not infringe on regular instructional activities.

5. Group therapy involving staged encounters, which are used to break down behaviors and defenses so that more effective reactions can be constructed, will be excluded from all curricular areas.

6. A survival game (an intellectual game that is played to stimulate moral and ethical thinking in individuals) puts people in hypothetical situations and causes them to make life-death decisions based on their values. The maturity level of public-school students is such that these games would be of little benefit and cause undue emotional stress and as such are invalid techniques to use in the public schools in Frederick County.

7. Sensitivity training, which involves encounter groups and in-depth analysis of personal feelings, shall not be practiced in the public schools in Frederick County.
   Sensitivity training is a type of experience-based learning. Participants work together in small groups over an extended period of time, learning through analysis of their own experiences, including feelings, reactions, perceptions, and behavior. One of the vehicles by which sensitivity training is con-

ducted is the T-group or encounter group.

8. Programs of a sensitive nature likely to generate legitimate public concerns should be screened by the appropriate subject area supervisor or director. It is the responsibility of the supervisor to determine the necessity of involving the Curriculum Committee of the Board of Education in judging the suitability of the material before approval is given.[5]

While these policies may or may not be appropriate for every community, they illustrate the way a local school board and a citizen group cooperated to formulate school policy.

BRIDGES THAT SPAN THE GAP

There are a number of bridges that may open the public schools to the teaching of religious points of view (including Christian) in the classroom. The following three programs have been defended by the Supreme Court. You may want to explore the possibility of one or more of these in your school system.

The Bible

The first bridge, approved by the Supreme Court in 1963 (in *Abington* v. *Schempp*) is the opportunity to teach the Bible *as literature* in the public school. The Supreme Court specifically declared in *Schempp*: "Nothing we have said here indicates that such study of the Bible or of religion, when presented objectively as part of a secular program of education, may not be effected consistent with the First Amendment."

"How can the Bible be taught in a public school?" you may ask. And how could you get kids to sign up for such a class if you had one?

The answers might surprise you. Dr. Joyce L. Vedral, an English teacher in a New York City high school, had the following experience when she initiated a course on the Bible as controversial literature, with her department's approval.

> Who would sign up for "Bible" if they saw it written on a paper? They would think it was either boring or "religious." So I determined to

go around and recruit students.

It was surprisingly easy. All I had to do was to appeal to their natural curiosity and to their sense of adventure. I gave a ten-minute speech in each of the English classes, announcing my name and the course I wanted to begin, and then plunging into questions such as: "Have you ever wondered who created God, or, how everything started if there is no God? Is there a devil? Who created him (it)? What does the Bible say about witchcraft? What does the Bible say happens after death? Do you agree with the Bible? Do you know that Jesus never said a word about sex before marriage?"

At this point the class would be in an uproar. All kinds of questions were hurled my way, and the teacher in charge of the class would try to restore order. "Calm down," I would say. "I can't deal with all of your questions now. You'll have to sign up for the course. At that time you'll have an opportunity to ask any question you want, and to express your own opinion on any issue you want. After we read the Bible, you can agree or disagree with it, and then you will have a chance to debate with priests, rabbis and ministers. They will come to the class and give their 'rap,' and after listening respectfully, you'll have a chance to question anything they say, yes, to ask those questions you could never ask in church or temple in the middle of a sermon."

I added, "In addition to all this, you will be reading the most quoted book in English literature, and you will greatly increase your insight into English literature. Also, it doesn't look half bad on a college transcript, if you've taken 'Bible as Literature.' "

After three days of recruiting, I had 500 students signed up. . . .[6]

Dr. Vedral explains that the main reason her school has

maintained the Bible course for nearly ten years now is that it works: students attend, get involved in the discussions, and learn. But the other important point is that the course *is* legal, and for several reasons. Vedral says:

> The Bible has influenced English literature more than any other book in the language. Without familiarity with the Bible, students hoping to go to college suffer a great disadvantage. Since few people in their teens (unfortunately) go to church on a regular basis, they have little or no knowledge of the Bible. For this reason, English departments are more than delighted to introduce courses in the Bible as literature.[7]

Another point in the class's favor is the teacher's non-partisan approach. Dr. Vedral regularly invites in speakers representing a number of different points of view on the Bible—and rarely takes a stand herself.

> I never tell the students that a particular miracle or doctrine is "true." Rather I discuss the biblical passage and ask for opinions. Then, at times, I give my opinion, adding that even I cannot prove it and that I base my opinion on many factors, faith included. The students love this approach because it frees them to think for themselves without guilt. . . .
>
> In the course we read the Bible stories to find the "principle" or "teaching" and discuss whether or not the individuals in the class agree with the principle.
>
> For example, a study of the story of Jacob and Esau demonstrates the principle of "reaping and sowing" or, "What goes around comes around" as the students reinterpret it. What you do comes back to you in the long run. Jacob deceived his brother Esau into selling him the birthright, and Jacob is later deceived by his father-in-law Laban, who tricks him into

marrying Leah, the wrong wife.

The class tosses it around. Do they agree?
Most of them seem to find evidence in their
own lives that what they do usually has repercussions.

We discuss the life of Abraham which
demonstrates the principle of faith. We delve
into the life of Joseph and analyze the element
of a "call" or a "destiny," discussing Joseph's
dreams.

Students volunteer stories of personal experiences involving faith or destiny or reaping
and sowing. Judy tells how she got a job by
faith. Paul tells how he knows he will be a
famous soccerplayer.[8]

A number of textbooks for the teaching of the Bible as
literature are available. *The Bible as Literature,* published by
Webster/McGraw-Hill (New York, N.Y.), divides the Bible for
study by literary form. The same approach is used in Leland
Ryken's *The Literature of the Bible* (Zondervan Publications,
Grand Rapids, Mich.), which is intended to be a college text, but
can serve as a high school teacher's resource. More student-
oriented are six shorter books on Bible literature themes: *Heroes
of Genesis, The Epic of the Exodus, Parables and Portraits of
the Bible, Poetry of the Bible, The Garden and the City,* and
Heroines of the Bible. These books each come with a teacher's
guide and are available from Mott Media, Inc. (100 East Huron,
Milford, MI 48042).

Another approach is the teaching of the Bible *in* literature—that is, looking at Bible stories and themes echoed in
later Western literary works. One textbook *The Bible as/in
Literature* (Scott, Foresman, & Co., Chicago, Ill.) does a bit of
both, using Bible passages and other pieces of literature relating
to the Bible.

Your local school may not wish to initiate an entire course
on the Bible—though it is just as valid as entire courses on
Shakespeare. If this is the case, English teachers could be encouraged to include portions of the Bible as part of a "Survey of
Western Literature" course.

Finally, Christians should not feel that studying the Psalms as poetry and the Book of Exodus as an ancient epic will take away the Scripture's power. God's Word will speak for itself to those who have not heard it before. And Christian students can gain new insights into the literary beauty of the Scriptures. The main problem with such a course might be the teacher's attitude. If the teacher has little sympathy for the content of the biblical story, the presentation might obviously be tainted by this bias.

Religion Classes

Another bridge is the teaching of comparative religion courses in public schools. Courses would, by definition, explain the history and tenets of a number of major religions of the world, and then let the students draw their own conclusions. This is natural in our pluralistic system. We should not be afraid to have the Christian faith held up as a "religion" and compared to the religions invented by man. With the Holy Spirit at work, such a class can have an impact, even if taught by a teacher who is not a Christian. Pastors and church members should be willing to help out teachers of such courses by suggesting supplemental texts for students researching Christianity, or by vounteering to appear as "guest lecturers."

Release Time Education

A final bridge to religious education is the opportunity for students to be released from school to attend religious instruction at another site such as a church. These programs are not new. Many of us were part of this type of Christian education in the late 1940s and the early 1950s. Often Catholic students were dismissed to catechism classes during the last hour of the school day and Protestants were permitted to attend release time programs.

The constitutionality of these programs was established in *Zorach* v. *Clauson* when the Supreme Court made this comment about release time programs:

> When the state encourages religious instruction or cooperates with religious authorities by adjusting the schedule of public events to sectarian needs, it follows the best of our traditions. For it then respects the religious nature of our people and accommodates the public ser-

> vice to their spiritual needs. To hold that it may
> not, would be to find in the Constitution a re-
> quirement that the government show a callous
> indifference to religious groups. That would be
> preferring those who believe in no religion over
> those who do believe.

Release time allows religious instruction that is intended to inform or convince students about a particular set of beliefs to be a part of the school day.

The religious groups in the community must initiate release time programs. Neither the local school nor the state can take any action that would "coerce anyone to attend church to observe a religious holiday, or to take religious instruction" (*Zorach* v. *Clauson*).

Often various religious groups, sects, and denominations form a common council, which provides both the structure and the administration for the program. However, each group maintains control over the location, materials, and religious content of its own course.

Because "no tax in any amount, large or small, can be levied to support any religious activities,"[9] the public schools cannot finance these release time programs. Parents or the religious groups must bear the costs, except for insignificant administrative expenses (such as those incurred from filing attendance reports).

And this type of program may be considered a credit course. It qualifies as custodial credit to fulfill the number of hours the state requires students to be in school. It may be considered for funding credit if the state's formula allows for such discretion. And the course may qualify as an elective credit toward a student's graduation.

Wait a minute, you might say. If the courses are elective credits, how much supervision may the public schools exercise over the content and teaching of these courses? Very little. Supervision might excessively entangle the state in religious matters. On the other hand, a school may inquire about the teacher's training or whether or not a particular course covers a subject for which credit can be given. This type of religious education might help to solve the quandary over religious and moral training in the secular schools. This process also avoids the problem of having an unsympathetic leader of a comparative religion or Bible as literature course.*

PRIVATE RELIGIOUS SCHOOLS

Obviously, concerned parents do have the opportunity to place their children in parochial or private Christian schools, where religion and morals are a valued part of a child's education. Approximately 11 percent of the nation's 48 million students attend private schools. Some educators even claim that the number of private religious schools in this country is growing at rates that exceed one new school every six hours.

A list of many of these schools can be found in the directory of *U.S. Christian Schools* by Cleveland C. Matchett or by writing one of the private religious school associations: the Association of Christian Schools International (ACSI), P.O. Box 4097, Whittier, CA 90607; the American Association of Christian Schools (AACS), 1017 N. School St., P.O. Box 587, Normal, IL 61761; the Christian Educators Association (CEA), 1101 Fuller Ave., SE, Grand Rapids, MI 49506; Board of Parish Education (Lutheran-Missouri Synod), 3558 S. Jefferson, St. Louis, MO 63118; and the National Catholic Educational Association, Suite 350, One Dupont Circle, Washington, D.C. 20036.

The cost of private education has kept some parents from sending their children to these schools. However, Reagan's new tuition tax credit program would open this sometimes expensive door to families with lower incomes. Reagan's program would allow a $500 credit for each child attending a private school if the parents' annual income was $50,000 or less. This program would be phased in over a three-year period: $100 or half the tuition (whichever is less) in 1983, $300 in 1984, and the full $500 by 1985. Tax credits are direct subtractions from the *taxes due*, so they amount to a 100 percent credit up to the limit provided.

A tax deduction plan for families who have children in private school has also been considered by some states. The relief is a tax deduction from state taxes, which is subtracted from the taxpayer's *total income* for the year rather than the *tax due*. This makes the credit relatively small. A family earning

*A monograph exploring the legal aspects of release time programs has been prepared by Samuel Ericsson of the Christian Legal Society, P.O. Box 2069, Oak Park, IL 60303.

$20,000 per year would only save $20.

The voucher plan is another approach to relief for private education. All parents in the United States would be given vouchers, which could be spent on whatever educational program they chose: public, parochial, or church school.

Any one of these plans is criticized by secular teachers' unions and educators who fear that encouraging private education might erode the already troubled public education system. The constitutionality of these proposals will probably be tested in the courts, so parents should not anticipate monetary relief in the near future. The battle for any aid to private education may be long and tedious.

LOVE KIDS

Finally, parents and educators alike must love their kids. In our amoral society children need love and affection more than ever. Suicide is the leading cause of death among teenagers. Between 1950 and 1975, the teen suicide rate jumped 171 percent among white youth from the ages of fifteen to nineteen. Professor Edward A. Wynne interpreted these statistics:

> The data not only portray increased alienation, they also raise important questions about the continuing vitality of American society. After all, that vitality ultimately depends upon the ability of adult-operated institutions such as schools to rear children and adolescents to become effective and competent adults.[10]

Wynne points to the self-centeredness and alienation of our youth, which in turn leads to loneliness and self-destruction.

How desperately we need effective homes and churches and schools! These factors cry out for a society that provides meaning, hope, and identity to youth—and all of us. How badly we need teachers and citizens who can truly love kids!

Christian teachers

Few professions have traditionally attracted as many Christians as school teaching, and today the ranks still include substantial numbers with commitments to teaching and their Christian faith. We need sharp, creative Christian teachers who are effective models for children. These teachers must not see their "Christian" role or witness simply in narrow terms of evangelism of fellow teachers or students. Surely their lives will invite those who observe them to consider the faith. But there is also a witness of Jesus Christ in contributing to the development of a solid educational program in a school and employing sensitive but firm discipline.

Too many teachers are paralyzed by their frustrations at what they may not do, and continually look for ways to "get around" prohibitions against teacher-led prayers or devotional Bible reading. We need teachers who are genuinely concerned about children developing moral character and learning essential skills. Christian teacher organizations must do more than encourage Christian teachers to resist destructive tendencies in education. They must work to equip their members to do a first-rate job in the schools of this country. The National Christian Educators Association is dedicated to equipping Christian teachers for effective work in public schools and expressing Judeo-Christian values in public school systems (for the association's address see p. 155).

Such a commitment is not likely to emerge until we see education as a ministry. Our preoccupation with clergy and missionaries as the only ones who are called to their task robs people in other disciplines of a biblical sense of vocation. God has placed teachers in the area of education as stewards, witnesses, and gifted and called persons.

There are so many things teachers and lay persons can do in education, and perhaps the most effective is to really care about learning and about children. There is indeed no Supreme Court case outlawing the exercise of this ministry. The ACLU will not sue. The principal will not have apoplexy nor the school board fear your action. Critics will largely be silenced. Children will seek your counsel.

Such lovers are desperately needed in education. We may not need more bureaucrats, more technologies, more new gimmicks, more specialists, and more union organizers. We need lovers. Not merely persons with smiles and "sweet talk," but lovers who encourage hard work and discipline. When such lovers speak of values and ethics and hope and faith, they may well elicit a very special response from their students. Who knows, the myth of the little red schoolhouse might even be fulfilled in the twentieth century by teachers and parents who truly love children.

16

Whoever Heard of Holy Terror?

"The instruments of Holy Terror in America must be disarmed. . . . Precedent would seem to compel the disestablishment of the electronic church, a paid religious broadcasting monopoly that has strayed beyond any reasonable notion of community service. . . .

"Political action committees that have in fact cobbled their platforms from scriptural, supernatural, sectarian or other religious dogma should be excluded from the political process for breaking the wall of separation between church and state. . . .

"And world evangelism by any group must be retired as a priority."

These statements, written by Flo Conway and Jim Siegelman in their book *Holy Terror,* form the basis of a battleground. What are the authors proposing? A total withdrawal of Christians from any influence on the environment in which we live. Just when Christians are beginning to vocally resist the secularization of education and American society, some persons are trying to deny our right to do so. *Holy Terror* seems to be just the beginning of a flood of books that seek to condemn Christian involvement in politics, government, and education.

But no volume more clearly expresses the growing hostility toward—and the ridicule of—an evangelical perspective than Conway's and Siegelman's book, whose subtitle is: "The Fundamentalist War on America's Freedom in Religion, Politics and Our Private Lives."

The authors claim that a "new terror" is sweeping our land, which seeks to "seize power" and "transform our culture into one altogether different from the one we have known." You may not realize it, but the authors probably see you as a part of this terrible conspiracy. Certainly they have included some of the most dedicated members of the evangelical community—the Wycliffe Bible translators, Bill Bright, director of Campus Crusade International, and the Navigators—as well as the more obvious choices, Jerry Falwell and Pat Robertson.

Conway and Siegelman are correct in noting that fundamentalists and evangelicals are now more politically active than they have been in decades. What has driven evangelical reverends and lay persons from their accustomed haunts to the halls of Congress?

Throughout this book we have suggested two important factors: a perception of a moral crisis in society and government, which threatens the fabric of our life, and, secondly, the development of a theology that requires Christians to become involved in the culture.

I don't think we can blame evangelicals for feeling that things are "not well in River City." In the second chapter I referred to the growing divorce rates, alcoholism, drug addiction, teenage suicides, abortions—all symptoms of the abandonment of traditional morality for an amoral life-style.

But if personal sin were the only cause for the evangelical's frustration, religious leaders would not be taking their crusade into courts and electoral districts. Instead they would concentrate on their own pulpits and reawaken preaching that would exhort individuals back to righteousness.

However, evangelicals perceive that the major social and political forces are willing co-conspirators in the assault on fundamental morality. The educational bureaucrats, the media moguls, the government in its courts, and the regulatory bureaucracies of our nation are seen as contributing to the moral crisis, both by omission and commission.

Schools are undisciplined, valueless, and shaped by relativism. The media fosters violence and exhalts immorality. Government has ceased to restrain evil.

Probably even the youngest of those reading this book remembers a time when the laws of almost every state provided penalties for homosexual conduct, pornography, and abortion.

Now the law has radically shifted its role. It has decriminalized, then given legal status to, and finally protected conduct it formerly prohibited.

But evangelicals have an even greater reason for speaking out on issues. There is a growing concern that the government is attacking the church and religious conscience in a direct assault on religious liberty. If this is true, the state will not only refuse to endorse your religious views, it will limit your right to exercise them. Some evangelicals are not only righteously indignant, they believe they are in a fight for freedom and survival.

Indeed, the very scope of cases working their way through the courts testifies to the fact that the state and religion are on different courses. Over three hundred cases were reported in 1981 by the Christian Legal Society in its publication, *Religious Freedom Reporter*. In the final issue of 1980, *U.S. News and World Report* recognized this collision. "The stage is set for a climactic confrontation over disputes of faith and statecraft."

A good part of the clash between church and state derives from the expansion of each sphere. Government tends to seek control and power, as perhaps any human institution does. Government, its laws, and its regulatory agencies invade our lives, control our businesses, and shape our schools. They assess. They demand. They codify. They regulate, certify, and license. They tax, aid, and insure. This expansiveness, combined with an often audacious claim, "The state is right; it has authority," is offensive to many with strong individualist traditions.

Above and beyond these changes in the environment in which we live, clergy and the pious have been driven from their churches and cloisters because of a new theological posture. It is a theology that rejects other-worldly pietism as an adequate response to discipleship and suggests that the arena of our ministry includes the present order, not just the hereafter. This theology also rejects any eschatology that suggests Christians can do nothing to change current events because they are a part of the end-time occurrences.

This new theology recognizes that salvation is more than just the individual's capacity to be born from above and experience the fullness of Christ's forgiveness and the indwelling of the Holy Spirit. Salvation also includes the promise in Ephesians that all creation will come to acknowledge God and find its unity in him. The salvation of the individual is just a part of God's intent to exercise his lordship over all of creation.

Lordship is perhaps the most comprehensive and revolutionary statement of the gospel. The word *Lord* is not, as so often seems the case, a name of endearment for Jesus or a synonym for *sweet* or *kind.* In the New Testament, *lord* is the Greek *kyrios,* which is cognate to *caesar, kaiser,* and *czar.* Sweet? By no means. Such persons are noted for power and authority. The word *Lord* recognizes the final and ultimate authority of Christ.

The Ephesian Christians did not anger the Romans or the worshippers of Diana because they preached the teachings of Jesus. Rome recognized many gods. But not one omnipotent God over all. Rome could not tolerate Jesus as *kyrios*—Lord— because this belief attacked Rome's final authority.

As long as evangelicals see Christ as Lord, they will resist the attempt to constrain their activities to what the secularist defines as "religion." Such persons offer us a certain territory: usually prayers, worship services, Bibles, gospel singing, and, of course, life after death.

Secularists seem to see twentieth century America as "my turf," and conflict always emerges when "my territory is invaded." In fact, Conway and Siegelman say America cannot "survive as two nations—one fundamentalist, one secular."

Of course they suggest that fundamentalists withdraw from the fray. But why should we withdraw when it would constrict the scope of our faith and undermine a moral and religious atmosphere that gives—and has given—health and vitality to our nation? Politics. Education. Art. Science. Philosophy. They are all part of the Christian's world.

Christians who are informed by the prophetic tradition of Elijah, Elisha, and Isaiah will not allow themselves to be isolated from the world. They will seek a structure that allows dialogue, engagement, judgment, and restoration. The right of free exercise will not be construed as merely creating an "off-limits" zone for Christians, but as creating the opportunity for churchmen to be full partners in the pluralism of our day.

Let's make secularists reevaluate the shibboleth "separation of church and state." The discussion or promotion of moral values that have religious origins does not tread on the boundaries of separation between church and state. Segments of the church have always taken postures they believed to be moral. The church is not suddenly stepping across some invisible boundary line when it speaks out about sexuality, abortion, or pornography.

Neither should secularists or the state be "out to get" the church for doing so. It is disturbing—even frightening—to see any attempt by government agents to use tax power to silence the church's moral teachings. For instance, one official of a state agency in California asked friends to note sermons in churches and comments by church officials on abortion and political issues so this information might be used to revoke tax exemption. Sound like America—or a totalitarian state?

And while we're speaking of totalitarian states, let's reject the contention that evangelicals are demagogues seeking to destroy the character of American liberty by creating a totalitarian state along their personal moral grounds. Yes, the pornographer would be restrained; the abortionist would not be funded by tax monies. Yes, there would be a return to state support for a more traditional moral code. But to compare that to the "witch-hunts" of Joseph McCarthy is less than accurate. After all, strong minorities on the Supreme Court and majorities in many state legislatures and the United States Congress once felt that laws restraining such activities were constitutional.

Much of the rhetoric against evangelicals is clearly unfounded. Certainly the authors of *Holy Terror* misrepresent Christianity when they accuse InterVarsity, the Navigators, and Campus Crusade of fostering "guerilla tactics" and promoting the religious idea of surrender, which, they claim, is the first secret of fundamentalism. Even the memorization of Scripture and instructions to obey the word of God are likened to cult indoctrination techniques.

But most frightening of all is the authors' call for an attack on "wildcat Bible-based Christian schools." Something must be done, they suggest, to save children from these horrible institutions that promote ignorance. The students' "minds are being shaped in their most formative years by a lesson plan that appears to teach contempt for reason and science, and condemnation of those who do not share the same religious beliefs or political views." The authors ask: "How can any group, in the complexity of our time, counsel its adherents in the act of surrendering the intellect, the emotions and the will—to anyone or anything?"

The answer seems rather obvious to me: If that someone is the omnipotent God who created the universe and whose Spirit lives in the heart of each of us, surrendering my intellect or will to him does not seem at all irrational. It seems quite natural.

Because of this type of Christian commitment, Conway and Siegelman suggest that the new fundamentalism must be understood in "clinical terms," an innuendo that seems to imply the kind of punitive hospitalization employed by Soviet Russia to "treat" its dissidents. One wonders what kind of terror, what kind of tyranny, Conway and Siegelman would create in order to divest us all of our ignorance and superstition.

I do not believe that an organized group of secular humanists is out to destroy the Christian influence in our culture and Christianity itself. But books like *Holy Terror* make me wonder. Certainly its authors are far too intelligent to have missed the real meaning of Christian doctrine. Christ is with us, not as a "living being" as they say we believe, but as the Spirit of the Lord within us. And certainly they must know that they are misusing the media themselves, just as they claim we are, by their exaggerations, innuendoes, and character assassinations.

We as Christians need to realize that many people see secular humanism as a compelling philosophy. And many are as committed to this philosophy as we are to Christianity. We need to be aware that some secularists are trying to erase moral and settled moral values from education and our society.

After all, it was not Jerry Falwell who declared, "Secular humanism has won out." It was Leo Pfeffer, the arch advocate of separation of church and state. And it was Paul Blanshard, another prominent separationist, who hailed the seventy-five years of his life as being years of increasing doubt—and then thanked education for diminishing his religious faith.

There is a struggle for the minds of men. If there is not—if there is no fundamental distinction between a biblical perspective and that of the secularist—then the whole biblical revelation is false. It consistently speaks of a struggle. A warfare.

Christians have every right to insist that the issue of whether or not God exists and is relevant to our lives is a question of urgency for our culture. Certainly the gods of man are dead. The Holocaust, a series of world wars, continuing prejudice, and intractable suffering expose the heresy that man can build a perfect world through his own knowledge and resources.

Leslie Fiedler observes the legacy we leave to our children:

> It's difficult to avoid the conclusion that western man has decided to abolish himself, creating his own boredom out of his affluence, his own vulnerability out of his strength, his own impotence out of his own erotomania. . . . At last, having educated himself into imbecility and polluted and drugged himself into stupefaction, he keels over, a weary, battered brontosaurus, and becomes extinct.

Is this the consequence of the materialism and existentialism exemplified in Neitzsche's declaration that God is dead? Can we exult with Nietzsche: "God is dead! God remains dead! And we have killed him. . . . Shall we not ourselves become gods. . . . There never was a greater event—and on account of it, all who are born after us belong to a higher history than any history hitherto!"?

Or can anyone glory in the singing of Algernon Swinburne's doxology in *The Hymn of Man?*

> Glory to Man in the highest
> For man is the master of things.

No! Empiricism, positivism, pragmatism, naturalism, instrumentalism—they are all empty. And man is empty. In such a world of emptiness, there is every right to introduce God. There is a God. A God of substance. And we are free to declare his judgment and salvation to twentieth century America.

Our right to do so is guaranteed to us by the First Amendent and our right to dissent, which is part of free speech. Even more fundamentally, this right is assured to us by the Declaration of Independence, which declares that these rights are "inalienable and endowed by our Creator"—not man. These rights are *not* given to us by the United States government. They are ours. We have *not* surrendered them to government. And we never will!

APPENDIX

NOTES

Chapter 1

1. *New York Times,* May 7, 1982, p. B10.

2. "Is School Prayer the Answer?" *U.S. News and World Report,* October 27, 1979, p. 291.

3. *New York Times,* April 8, 1979, p. 1.

4. "Is School Prayer the Answer?" *Commonweal,* May 21, 1982, p. 291.

5. *New York Times,* May 7, 1982, p. B10.

Chapter 2

1. Frank Goble, *Beyond Failure: How to Cure a Neurotic Society* (Ottawa: Green Hill Publishers, 1977), p. 19.

2. Ibid., p. 20.

3. Ibid., p. 22.

4. U.S., Congress, House, Sub-Committee on Courts, Civil Liberties, *Hearing on S. 450,* 96th Cong., July 29-30, August 19-21, September 9, 1980.

5. "Matters Have Gotten out of Hand in a Violent Society," *U.S. News and World Report,* June 28, 1982, p. 49-50.

6. "End of the Permissive Society," *U.S. News and World Report,* June 28, 1982, p. 48.

7. Richard Neuhaus, "Who, Now, Will Shape the Meaning of America?" *Christianity Today,* March 19, 1982, pp. 18-19.

8. "Is School Prayer the Answer?" *Commonweal,* May 21, 1982, p. 291.

9. Kevin Phillips, "New Right and New Hysteria," *Good News,* January/February 1982, p. 35.

10. George Beadle, "Genes, Culture and Man," *Columbia University Forum,* VIII, no. 3 (Fall 1965) as quoted in Goble, *Beyond Failure,* p. 27.

11. Lawrence Brewer, "The Falling Away from Public Schools," *The Christian Citizen,* September 1981, p. 32f.

12. Ibid., p. 32.

13. Rudolf Flesch, "Why Johnny Can't Read," *U.S. News and World Report,* September 7, 1981, pp. 50-52.

14. Paul Copperman, *The Literacy Hoax: The Decline of Reading, Writing & Learning in the Public Schools & What We Can Do About It* (New York: William Morrow & Co., Inc., 1978), pp. 17, 175.

15. Stanley N. Wellborn, "Are Public Schools About to Flunk?" *U.S. News and World Report,* June 8, 1981, p. 59.

16. "School House Blues," *New Republic,* April 18, 1981, p. 8.

17. *Washington Post,* August 31, 1976.

18. "So Much for Innocence: The Evils of the NEA," *Bristol Herald Courier,* January 24, 1982.

19. Ibid.

Chapter 3

1. Sidney B. Simon, Leland W. Howe, and Howard Kirschenbaum, *Values Clarification: A Handbook for Practical Strategies for Teachers and Students,* (New York: Hart Publishing Co., 1972), p. 20.

2. Ibid., p. 46.

3. Rockne McCarthy, et al., *Society, State, and the Schools* (Grand Rapids, Mich.: Eerdmans: 1981). *See* also Peter B. Dow, "MACOS: The Study of Human Behavior as One Road to Survival," *Phi Delta Kappan,* October 1975, p. 80; and Susan Marshall, *Man: A Course of Study—Prototype for Federalized Textbooks?* (Washington, D.C.: Heritage Foundation, 1975), p. 3.

4. *Wall Street Journal,* April 12, 1982, p. 24.

5. Martin Eger, "The Conflict in Moral Education: An Informal Case Study," *The Public Interest,* Spring 1981, p. 62.

6. *Wall Street Journal,* April 12, 1982, p. 24

7. Ibid.

8. Ibid.

9. Ibid.

10. Ibid.

11. Frances Adeney, "Some Schools Are Looking East for Answers," *Moody Monthly,* May 1982, pp. 18-20.

12. Ibid., p. 19.

13. Ibid.

14. *Los Angeles Times,* March 28, 1980, p. 1.

15. Onalee McGraw, *The Family, Feminism and the Therapeutic State* (Washington, D.C.: The Heritage Foundation, 1980), p. 15-16.

16. Jeane Westin, *The Coming Parent Revolution* (Chicago: Rand McNally, 1981) p. 221.

17. Ibid.

18. Rhoda Lorand, "The Betrayal of Youth," *Education Update,* vol. 3, no. 3 (1979), p. 7-8.

19. Donald Oppewal, "Christian Textbooks? Yes!" *Christian Education Journal,* April 1972, pp. 7-8.

20. Harold Pflug, "Religion in Missouri Textbooks," *Phi Delta Kappan,* April 1955, p. 260.

21. George Hillocks, "Books and Bombs: Ideological Conflict and the Schools," *School Review,* August 1982.

22. *Congressional Record,* December 14, 1974, p. 18.

23. Scott Thomson, "High Stakes in Matter of Censorship," *Education Week,* May 19, 1982.

24. Allan Glatthorn, as quoted in "Censorship and the Public Schools: Who Decides What Students Will Read?" *Education Update,* vol. 6, no. 3 (July 1982), p. 3.

25. *Tucson Citizen,* March 26, 1982, p. 16.

Chapter 4

1. Paul Blanshard, *Religion and the Schools: The Great Controversy* (Boston: Beacon Press, 1963).

2. Arthur E. Sutherland, Jr., "Establishment According to Engel," *Harvard Law Review* 76, no. 1 (November 1962): 45.

3. *New York Times,* January 9, 1952.

4. *Peekskill Evening Star,* January 16, 1952.

5. Blanshard, *Religion and the Schools,* p. 33.

6. "The Supreme Court: To Stand as a Guarantee," *Time,* July 6, 1962, p. 7.

7. *Washington Post,* July 7, 1962.

8. "The Court Decision—and the School Prayer Furor," *Newsweek,* July 9, 1962, pp. 43-45.

9. Blanshard, *Religion and the Schools.*

10. *New York Times,* July 1, 1962.

11. Charles E. Rice, *The Supreme Court and Public Prayer: The Need for Restraint* (New York: Fordham University Press, 1964), pp. xi, xii.

12. "What's Being Said About Court's Rulings?" *U.S. News and World Report,* July 9, 1962, p. 44.

13. "The Court Decision—and the School Prayer Furor," *Newsweek,* July 9. 1962, pp. 43-45.

14. "Paradoxes in Legal Logic," *Life,* July 13, 1962, p. 4.

15. "Another Kind of Defiance," *Time,* August 24, 1962, p. 40.

Chapter 5

1. *New York Times,* June 6, 1962, p. 17.

2. Ibid.

3. "The Supreme Court, 1962 Term," *Harvard Law Review* 77 (1963): 63.

4. William J. Murray, *My Life without God* (Nashville, Tenn.: Thomas Nelson Publishers, 1982), pp. 47-48.

5. Andrew Farley, "A Trilogy: Engel, Murray and Schempp: The Supreme Court and Public School Devotions," *Union Seminary Quarterly Review* 19 no. 1 (November 1963): 24, 25.

6. Leo Pfeffer, *Church, State, and Freedom,* rev. ed. (Boston: Beacon Press, 1967), p. 445.

7. William K. Muir, Jr., *Prayer in the Public Schools: Law and Attitude Change* (Chicago: University of Chicago Press, 1967).

8. M. R. Konvitz, *Expanding Liberties* (New York: Viking Press), p. 45.

9. Pfeffer, *Church,* p. 475.

10. Ibid., p. 450.

11. Blanshard, *Religion and the Schools.*

12. "Nation Chooses Sides in Fight over Prayer," *U.S. News and World Report,* May 18, 1964, pp. 63, 64.

13. *New York Times,* January 30, 1964.

14. Kenneth Dolbeare and Philip Hammond, *The School Prayer Decisions: From Court to Local Practice,* (Chicago: University of Chicago Press, 1971).

15. David Lawrence, "The Right to Pray," *U.S. News and World Report,* March 2, 1964, p. 96.

16. Emmet John Hughes, "Schoolroom and Prayers," *Newsweek,* July 1, 1963, p. 15.

17. "What's Being Said About Court's Rulings?" *U.S. News and World Report,* July 9, 1962, p. 44.

18. "What About the Becker Amendment?" *Christianity Today,* June 19, 1964, p. 20.

19. *Congressional Digest* 43 (November 1964): 257-288.

Chapter 6

1. *New York Times,* April 20, 1980, Education, p. 3.

2. "And It Came to Pass," *National Review,* February 22, 1980, p. 201.

3. *Louisiana Revised Statutes,* Title 17, sec. 2115 (B).

4. U.S., Congress, Senate, *Congressional Record,* 97th Cong., 2d sess., 1980.

5. Ibid., 97th Cong., 1st sess., 1980.

6. U.S., Congress, House, Committee on the Judiciary, *Hearing on S.1577,* 97th Cong., 1st sess.

7. Scott Slonim, "Say Dormant Prayer Bill Has Broad Implications," *American Bar Association Journal* 66 (1980): 437.

8. U.S., Congress, House, Sub-Committee on Courts, Civil Liberties, *Hearing on S.450,* 96th Cong., July 29-30; August 19-21; Sept. 9, 1980.

9. J. Elliot Corbett, "Prayer in the Public Schools," *Engage / Social Action,* vol. 8, no. 10 (December 1980): 6.

10. *Civil Liberties,* May 1982, p. 4.

11. Raoul Berger, "Congressional Contraction of Federal Jurisdiction," *Wisconsin Law Review,* vol. 1980, no. 4 (September / October 1980):801ff.

12. Ibid., pp. 809-810.

Chapter 7

1. Charles E. Rice, *The Supreme Court and Public Prayer: The Need for Restraint* (New York: Fordham University Press, 1964).

2. Ordinance of 1787, July 13, 1787, article 3.

3. Walter Berns, *The First Amendment and the Future of American Democracy* (New York: Basic Books 1976), p. 13.

4. Thomas Jefferson, "Notes on the State of Virginia," *Works,* vol. 4 (New York: Putnam Books, 1904-5): 83.

5. Madalyn Murray O'Hair, *Freedom Under Siege: The Impact of Organized Religion on Your Liberty and Your Pocketbook,* (Los Angeles: J.P. Tarcher, Inc., 1974), p. 35.

6. Sidney Hook, *Religion in a Free Society,* (Lincoln, Nebr.: University of Nebraska Press, 1967), p. 59.

7. "Comment: The Supreme Court, The First Amendment and Religion in the Public Schools," Columbia Law Review 63, no. 1. (1963): p. 75.

8. Rice, *Supreme Court and Public Prayer.*

9. *Congressional Digest* 43 (November 1964): 280.

10. Pfeffer, *Church,* pp. 86-88.

11. James M. Dunn, "Reflections," *Report from the Capitol* 37, no. 5 (May 1982), p. 15.

12. Murray O'Hair, *Supreme Court, First Amendment and Religion,* p. 31.

13. Ibid.

14. Andrew Farley, "A Trilogy: Engel, Murray and Schempp: The Supreme Court and Public School Devotions," *Union Seminary Quarterly Review* 19, no. 1 (November 1963): 27.

Chapter 8

1. U.S., Congress, Senate, Sub-Committee on Courts, Civil Liberties, and the Administration of Justice of the Committee on the Judiciary, *Hearing on S.450,* 96th Cong., 2d sess., 1980, p. 9.

2. Richard Cohen, "A Child's Choice Is Not Voluntary," *Civil Liberties,* May 1982, p. 7.

3. Charles E. Rice, *The Supreme Court and Public Prayer: The Need for Restraint* (New York: Fordham University Press, 1964), p. 107.

4. "To Our Jewish Friends," *America,* September 1, 1962.

5. Institute of Church and State: *Proceedings* vols. 3, 4 (University of Villanova School of Law, 1963): 79, 80.

6. Rice, p. ix.

Chapter 9

1. Frederick Hochwalt, "A Catholic Educator's View," *American Education and Religion,* ed. F. Ernest Johnson, p. 68.

2. Charles E. Rice, *The Supreme Court and Public Prayer: The Need for Restraint* (New York: Fordham University Press, 1964), p. x.

3. Paul G. Kauper, *Religion and the Constitution* (Baton Rouge, La.: Louisiana State University Press, 1964), p. 32.

4. Franky Schaeffer, "The Myth of Neutrality," *Moody Monthly,* November 1980, pp. 20, 22.

5. Kauper, *Religion and the Constitution,* p. 31.

6. Frank Sheed, *Society and Sanity* 7 (1953), p. 7.

7. Donald Gianella, "Religious Liberty, Non-Establishment, and Doctrinal Development Part II," *Harvard Law Review* 81, no. 3 (January 1968): 561.

8. Donald E. Boles, *The Bible, Religion and the Public Schools* (Ames, Iowa: Iowa State University Press, 1963), p. 9.

9. Pfeffer, *Church,* p. 285.

10. Madalyn Murray O'Hair, *Freedom Under Siege: The Impact of Organized Religion on Your Liberty and Your Pocketbook* (Los Angeles: J.P. Tarcher, Inc., 1974).

11. Ibid., p. 98.

12. Boles, *Bible and Public Schools,* p. 205.

13. Pfeffer, *Church,* p. 375.

14. Paul Blanshard, *Religion and the Schools,* p. 19.

15. Ray Billington, *The Protestant Crusade* (New York: Macmillan Co., 1938), pp. 231, 295.

16. F. Ernest Johnson, "Statement of the Problem," *American Education and Religion: The Problem of Religion in the Schools* (Port Washington, N.Y.: Kennikat Press, Inc., 1952), p. 12.

17. Nicholas F. Gier, "Humanism as an American Heritage," *Free Inquiry,* Spring 1982, p. 27.

18. *Wall Street Journal,* February 22, 1982, p. 22.

19. Ibid.

Chapter 10

1. *Christian Legal Society Quarterly,* vol. 1, no. 4 (1980), p. 15.

2. Doug Willis, "Curb Says ACLE Is a Force that Lobbies for Criminals," *Vision,* vol. 27, no. 9 (1982): p. 27.

3. Ibid.

4. Charles Markman, *The Noblest Cry* (New York: St. Martin's Press, 1965), p. 1.

5. Peggy Lamson, *Roger Baldwin* (Boston: Houghton Mifflin, 1976), p. 86.

6. Ibid., p. 91.

7. Ibid., p. 141.

8. Ibid., p. 187.

9. Ibid., pp. 190-191.

10. Ibid., p. 183.

11. Ibid., p. 125.

12. Frank J. Sorauf, "Wall of Separation," *The Constitution Politics of Church and State* (Princeton, N.J.: Princeton University Press, 1976).

Chapter 11

1. Vivian T. Thayer, "An Experimentalist Position," *American Education,* p. 19.

2. Inscription on the Jefferson Memorial, Washington, D.C.

3. Charles E. Rice, *The Supreme Court and Public Prayer: The Need for Restraint* (New York: Fordham University Press, 1964), pp. xi, xii.

4. *Congressional Digest* 43 (November 1964): 270.

5. Sidney Hook, *Religion in a Free Society* (Lincoln, Nebr.: University of Nebraska Press, 1967), p. 21.

6. "Return Prayer to Public Schools?" *U.S. News and World Report* 89, no. 11 (1980): 69, 70.

7. Thayer, *American Education,* p. 27.

8. Leon Jaworski, *Crossroads* (Elgin, Ill.: David C. Cook Publishing Co., 1981), pp. 206-207.

9. Reinhold Kerstan, *Blood and Honor* (Elgin, Ill.: David C. Cook Publishing Co., 1980), p. 99.

10. Arthur E. Sutherland, Jr., "Establishment According to Engel," Harvard Law Review 76, no. 1 (November 1962): 51.

11. "Furor over School Prayers—Latest in a Growing Debate," *U.S. News and World Report,* May 11, 1964, pp. 72-74.

12. W. Hubert Porter, "For the Record: A Denominational Official on the Prayer Decision," *Foundations* 6, no. 1 (January 1963): 91.

13. George F. Will, "Opposing Pre-Fab Prayer," *Newsweek,* June 7, 1982, p. 84.

14. Ibid.

15. Leo Trepp, "An Exercise in Futility," *Liberty,* November/ December 1980, pp. 6-7.

16. *Christian Science Monitor,* April 20, 1979, p. 22.

17. John Warwick Montgomery, "School Prayers: A Common Danger," *Christianity Today,* May 7, 1982, p. 59.

Chapter 12

1. Richard V. Pierard, "As We See It," *Reformed Journal,* July 1981, p. 3.

2. Ibid., p. 2.

3. Learned Hand, *Spirit of Liberty* (New York: Vantage Books, 1959), p. 144.

Chapter 14

1. Howard Means, "Let Us Now Buy the Public Schools," *The Washingtonian,* May 1981, pp. 89-93.

2. Frank Gaebelein, as quoted in George Van Alstine, *The Christian and the Public School* (Nashville, Tenn.: Abingdon, 1982), p. 68.

3. William Raspberry, *Washington Post,* May 17, 1978.

4. Ethel Herr, "Schools: How Parents Can Make a Difference" (Chicago: Moody Press, 1981), p. 71.

5. John Fentriss Gardner, *The Experience of Knowledge* (Garden City, N.Y.: Waldorf Press, 1978), p. 216.

6. George Weigel, "A Symposium on Christianity and Democracy," *The Center Journal,* vol. 1, no. 3 (1982): 72.

7. C. S. Lewis, *The Abolition of Man* (New York: Macmillan, 1962), p. 35.

8. "Our Children Are Treated Like Idiots," *Psychology Today,* July 1981, p. 34.

9. Wolfgang Kohler, *The Place of Value in a World of Facts* (New York: Liveright Publishing Co., 1938), pp. 7-10.

10. David Little, "*Pierce* and the Religion Clauses: Some Reflection in Summary," *Freedom and Education:* Pierce *v.* Society of Sisters *Reconsidered* (Notre Dame, Ind.: University of Notre Dame Law School, 1978), p. 75.

Chapter 15

1. Westin, *The Coming Parent Revolution,* p. 32.

2. Ibid.

3. Ibid.

4. Ibid.

5. Frederick Post, as quoted in Onalee McGraw, *Secular Humanism and the Schools: The Issue Whose Time Has Come* (Washington, D.C.: The Heritage Foundation, 1976), pp. 12-17.

6. Joyce Vedral, "I Teach Bible in a Public School," *Christian Herald,* September 1982, p. 12.

7. Ibid., p. 18.

8. Ibid., p. 16.

9. Edward A. Wynne, "Behind the Discipline Problem: Youth Suicide as a Measure of Alienation," *Phi Delta Kappan,* January 1978, pp. 307-315.